A BUSY DAY

T0258338

Fanny Burney

A BUSY DAY

Adapted by Alan Coveney

OBERON BOOKS
LONDON

WWW.OBERONBOOKS.COM

First published in 2000 by Oberon Books Ltd
521 Caledonian Road, London N7 9RH
Tel: +44 (0) 20 7607 3637 / Fax: +44 (0) 20 7607 3629
e-mail: info@oberonbooks.com
www.oberonbooks.com

A catalogue record for this book is available from the British
Library.

ISBN: 978-1-84002-175-2

Cover illustration by Free Barabbas

CONTENTS

INTRODUCTION

Fanny Burney (1752-1840) was the most popular woman novelist of her day. The darling of Dr Johnson, admired by Jane Austen, all four of her novels were best sellers. In this century she is better known as a diarist. Her vivid accounts of late eighteenth and early nineteenth century drawing-room life have never been out of print. A reluctant Keeper of the Robes to Queen Charlotte, she was famously chased around Kew Gardens by the mad King George III. At the age of 41 she married a French émigré and her letters include a chilling account of undergoing a mastectomy without anaesthetic at the hands of Napoleon's surgeons.

But unknown to most people, Burney also wrote plays, four tragedies and four comedies, of which *A Busy Day* is undoubtedly the finest. Encouraged by Dr Johnson, Sheridan and others to write for the theatre, there is no doubt that Burney intended her plays for performance. However, in her own lifetime, her ambitions as a playwright were constantly thwarted by prejudice, incompetence or historical accident.

Forced by her censorious, authoritarian father to abandon two of her earlier plays, and embarrassed by the fiasco of a verse tragedy, *Edwy and Elgiva*, which played for only one night in 1795, Burney nevertheless started work on two new plays in the late 1790s. One of them was *A Busy Day* . The play's vigour and energy and fundamental optimism seem to reflect her own mood at the time – in love, newly married, a mother for the first time, and free at last from her father's narrow-minded prejudice.

This time, however, it was international events that got in the way. In 1802, during a lull in the Napoleonic Wars, Burney crossed to France to join her husband, taking with her their young son and the manuscripts of her plays. Almost immediately war between England and France was resumed and the family were trapped in exile for ten years. By the time she returned to England, Burney had a growing son to provide for, her husband was still in France and she had written a fourth novel. This was no time to reinvent herself as a playwright. The manuscript of

A Busy Day, so lovingly transcribed by her husband during their time in France, was consigned to the bottom of her trunk.

Late in her life Burney undertook the task of editing her "immense Mass of Manuscripts" as she called them. She destroyed some material for personal reasons, but most of it she itemised and arranged with notes and dates, leaving an invaluable account of late eighteenth century middle class life. She leaves no record of what she thought of her plays, or whether she had any hopes for their future, but she must have come upon her manuscript for *A Busy Day* during these years and decided, thankfully, to leave it intact.

Until very recently the play existed only in manuscript, available to scholars as part of the Berg Collection in the New York Public Library, but not really accessible to those interested in performing the work. I hope that this edition will finally bring this wonderful play to a wider audience.

Alan Coveney
Bristol, 2000

A Busy Day received its first ever performance at the Hen and Chicken Pub Theatre, North Street, Bristol on 29 September 1993, produced by Show of Strength Theatre Company. The cast was as follows:

Lord John Dervis	BRENDAN HOOPER
Sir Marmaduke Tylney	JAMES CLARKSON
Lady Wilhelmina Tylney	HELEN WEIR
Cleveland	RICHARD STEMP
Frank Cleveland	IAN KELLY
Jemima Cleveland	CLAIRE MACAULAY
Miss Percival	JULIETTE GRASSBY
Mr. Watts	GEOFFREY COLLINS
Mrs. Watts	CAROLINE HUNT
Peggy	MAGGIE O'BRIEN
Eliza	WENDY HEWITT
Joel Tibbs	PAUL NICHOLSON
Deborah	HELEN WEIR
Waiter, Valet & Servant	DAVID TAYLOR
Director	ALAN COVENEY
Designer	ELIZABETH BOWDEN
Costume Design	MAGGIE CHAPELHOW

The first London West End production opened at the Lyric Theatre, Shaftesbury Avenue on 19 June 2000; a Bristol Old Vic production presented by Julius Green & Ian Lenagan. The cast was as follows:

Lord John Dervis	BEN MOOR
Sir Marmaduke Tylney	JOHN McCALLUM
Lady Wilhelmina Tylney	STEPHANIE BEACHAM
Cleveland	SIMON ROBSON
Frank Cleveland	IAN KELLY
Jemima Cleveland	OLGA SOSNOVSKA
Miss Percival	SARA CROWE
Mr. Watts	RICHARD KANE
Mrs. Watts	CAROL MACREADY
Peggy	CAROLYN BACKHOUSE
Eliza	SARA MARKLAND
Joel Tibbs	ROBERT DEMEGER
Deborah	STEPHANIE FAYERMAN
Waiter, Valet & Servant	MILO TWOMEY
Director	JONATHAN CHURCH
Designer	RUARI MURCHISON
Lighting Designer	NICK BEADLE

CHARACTERS

LORD JOHN DERVIS
Second son of the Marquis of W.

SIR MARMADUKE TYLNEY
A landowner in London for the Season.

LADY WILHELMINA TYLNEY
His childless second wife.

GEORGE CLEVELAND
Sir Marmaduke's nephew & just returned from India.

FRANK CLEVELAND
His younger brother & friend to Lord John.

JEMIMA CLEVELAND
Their sister.

MISS PERCIVAL
A wealthy heiress.

MR. WATTS
Rich and now retired from business.

MRS. WATTS
His wife.

PEGGY
Their daughter.

ELIZA
Their younger daughter, raised in India since a child.

JOEL TIBBS
Cousin to Mr Watts.

DEBORAH
Eliza's servant.

WAITER

VALET

SERVANTS

A NOTE ABOUT THE TEXT

This text has been edited and adapted for theatre production. Having been unperformed for 200 years I wanted an edition that could be used by actors and directors in the rehearsal room as well as read by general readers.

Adaptation can present difficult choices for the editor. Although an enthusiastic theatre goer, Burney was not an experienced dramatist. The manuscript of *A Busy Day* was like a first draft which needed to be honed by the rigours of the rehearsal process. For the most part my approach has been that of a sympathetic script editor – cutting unnecessary repetition, telescoping events, shortening expositions (which were needed in the eighteenth century when each act might be followed by an interval). It would have been wonderful to commission some re-writes from the author, but I was two centuries too late. As far as was possible, every word in this edition was written by Fanny Burney.

A reviewer in The Financial Times commented after seeing the play: "I suspect such astonishingly Wildean remarks as "One has no chance with any girl until her family are all against one" owe more to the adaptor than Miss Burney." I am glad to say that not only those lines, but also the whole of that particular scene, are one hundred percent uncut, unedited Burney.

I have followed the first printed version of the text edited by Tara Ghoshal Wallace, which regularizes certain inconsistencies of capitalisation and puntuation, but largely retains the spelling of the manuscript. The peculiarities of grammar and spelling I think add to the period feel of the play but are never so strange to a modern ear as to confuse the meaning.

The original manuscript of *A Busy Day* is part of the Berg Collection of the New York Public Library.

Alan Coveney
Bristol, 2000

ACT I

London, 1800. Early morning. An apartment in a Gentlemen's Gambling Club in St. James' St.

1ST VOICE: *(Outside.)* There! there! open that door! To the right I say!

2ND VOICE: It's bespoke.

1ST VOICE: Open it, I say! the lady's fainting – open it, when I bid you.

A door opens, and ELIZA bursts in, with her servant DEBORAH, and a WAITER carrying a large trunk.

DEBORAH: Take care, take care, my dear young lady! O that Mr Cleveland was but with us!

ELIZA: Hush, hush, good Deborah! why are you so alarm'd! I am not hurt, I assure you.

DEBORAH: O, you don't know yet – nor I neither; but I dare say I'm bruised all over, when I come to examine. Mercy on us what a thing to travel so many thousands and thousands and millions of miles only to be overturned at last! If Mr Cleveland had but been with us –

ELIZA: Be quiet, dear Deborah. Pray where are we now? *(To the WAITER.)* I am entirely a stranger to London.

WAITER: In St James' Street, meme. I thought nobody so ignorant as that! *(Aside.)*

ELIZA: How far are we from Bond Street?

WAITER: Just by, meme.

ELIZA: Can you procure me a carriage to convey one thither?

WAITER: O dear, yes, meme.

ELIZA: See for one, then, I beg. And pray assist my servant in taking care of my trunks.

WAITER: What, the Black?

ELIZA: Yes; be so good as to see if he wants any help.

WAITER: What, the Black?

ELIZA: Yes. I shall be extremely concerned if he should meet with any accident. See if you can be of any use to him.

WAITER: What, the Black?

ELIZA: Yes. I shall be much obliged to you for any service you may do him. Pray make haste.

WAITER: Certainly, meme. Good Lord!

Exit sneering.

ELIZA: Poor Ranjit! my care of you shall be trebled for the little kindness you seem likely to meet with here.

Enter CLEVELAND.

CLEVELAND: My beloved Eliza!

DEBORAH: Mercy on us! if here i'n't Mr Cleveland his own self!

ELIZA: Cleveland!

CLEVELAND: What a terrible accident!

ELIZA: It was but the panic of a moment. I escaped all injury. But how can you have heard –

DEBORAH: O Mr Cleveland! that ever my dear young lady sent you away from us. We've had nothing but the ill luck of being broke down and overturned ever since: and I don't know yet half how bad I am; but I dare say –

CLEVELAND: Dear Mrs Deborah, will you have the kindness to ask Ranjit if the baggage is all right?

DEBORAH: Ay, ay, Mr Cleveland, I understand you well enough! you've only a mind to get rid of me, that you may say pretty things to my dear young lady here. As if you could not just as well say 'em before me. I warrant you suppose I have never had a sweetheart myself. Lord help your poor young heads both of you!

Exit.

CLEVELAND: I must at least confess her penetration to be less deficient than her delicacy. My dearest Eliza! *(Kissing her hand.)* how anxiously –

ELIZA: Tell me, I beseech you, by what chance you were in this house? By what chance you discovered –

CLEVELAND: I was not in this house; nor must you, my Eliza, one unnecessary moment remain in it. Though nominally an Hotel, it is, in fact, a notorious Gaming House.

ELIZA: Let me, then, hasten from it instantly. I have sent for some carriage –

CLEVELAND: Send rather for your Family; – unless, indeed, you will accept me as a guard to convey you to them.

ELIZA: Not for the Universe! ignorant of our connexion, what could they think of seeing me with a Guardian so little... venerable?

CLEVELAND: But Mr Alderson himself made over to me the tenderest as well as most solemn powers of protection.

ELIZA: But they are uninformed of his sanction, and after an absence of the greatest part of my life – will it not appear like triumphing in my independence?

CLEVELAND: I will not oppose an impulse which I revere. But tell me what circumstances –

ELIZA: We arrived in perfect safety; but as we passed just opposite to this house, the chaise broke down. But let me write to my Father; I will then explain how it happened.

CLEVELAND: Is there no bell in this room? Here! Waiter!

Enter WAITER who has been listening at the door.

WAITER: Your commands, sir?

CLEVELAND: A pen and ink for this lady.

ELIZA: And pray be so good as to contradict the orders I gave for a carriage.

WAITER: A carriage, meme?

ELIZA: Yes; I begged you to let me have one immediately.

WAITER: Did you, meme? What wine did you say, sir?

CLEVELAND: Wine? I said pen and ink.

WAITER: Pen and ink, sir?

CLEVELAND: Yes; make haste.

WAITER: Certainly, sir. I wonder I don't. Pen and ink, indeed!

Aside, and exit loiteringly.

CLEVELAND: Whoever comes hither but for wine, or for dice, is only in the way.

Enter DEBORAH.

DEBORAH: Well, I suppose I come too soon, according to the old story; but Ranjit is safe, and the trunks are safe, and so –

CLEVELAND: Will you, then, have the goodness to get your lady a pen and ink?

DEBORAH: Now that's fudge again, just to get me off! Why I tell you, I should like to hear what you're to say as well as yourselves.

CLEVELAND: This is too fatiguing! I will be back instantly.

Exit.

DEBORAH: There, now! if he had not rather fetch the pen and ink himself, than talk to you before me! And here he is already! I believe he deals with a conjurer.

Re-enter CLEVELAND.

CLEVELAND: I have seized this from the adjoining room.

ELIZA: A thousand thanks.

She seats herself at a table and writes.

DEBORAH: If you'll believe me Mr Cleveland if it had not been for my old master Mr Alderson's promising to be the making of me, if I'd take care of my dear young lady here across those seas, I'd no more have gone to the land's end, there, than I'd have flown in the air. But what my young lady sent you off for, as soon as we got on dry land, I don't know; for lord! as to being so afraid to let people see one's got a sweetheart. I never minded it, for my part, when it was my own case. And I don't know that I should now, if it was to happen to me over again.

ELIZA: Deborah, pray find a messenger.

DEBORAH: Ay, ay; I'll go. If I can't make sport, at least I won't spoil it. "To Thomas Watts, Esquire Bond Street." Well, I'll warrant you an answer in ten minutes. So talk fast; for I suppose they must not hear you no more than I. Lover's whims, lord help 'em! However, I've had my own. And nobody knows but what I may have 'em again.

Exit.

ELIZA: Tell me, now, by what means –

CLEVELAND: When I left you, as so rigidly you commanded, at Portsmouth, a thousand nameless fears prevented my proceeding, and I loitered, that, at least at every change of horses, I might gather news of your safety. But when I found, at Guildford, that you continued your journey alone, I ordered my driver to pursue your chaise at once. Imagine, then, my horror, to see it overturned in the street! And then to find you were come into this House!

ELIZA: You must not reproach my desire of a short separation. It is only that my Family may hear the history of our engagement before you meet them.

CLEVELAND: But when will you permit me to present myself?

ELIZA: When you have written to my Father. A line will suffice to make an opening. I will then completely develop the whole history: but I shall never have the courage to begin the subject. His consent, his approbation cannot be doubted. Your high family, their rank in life, and your noble connexions, will make him proud of such an alliance, and of the honour which it will reflect upon his Daughter.

CLEVELAND: Generous, noble Eliza! from you springs all of honour the connexion can boast; for what is honour if its source is not virtue? How do I now bless the parsimonious reserve of my uncle, which compelled my Indian expedition! Without it, I had never known my Eliza!

ELIZA: I long to hear the motive that has caused his so sudden recall!

CLEVELAND: I cannot have any doubt but it is to announce me at length, openly for his heir. He would else certainly not have broken up, in so peremptory a manner, the rising promises of my own industry.

Enter DEBORAH.

DEBORAH: Well, I hope I've stayed away long enough now? Though I can't say you look very glad to see me. But as the Porter said he'd be back in five minutes, I thought it best to give you a hint, for ten of them are over already.

ELIZA: O hasten away, then, I beseech you! you must not add the confusion of an explanation of this nature, to the perturbation of a meeting so affecting to my heart. I entreat you to begone!

CLEVELAND: Retain your firmness my Eliza! I obey.

Kisses her hand, and exit.

DEBORAH: He takes her hand with a very pretty air, that's the truth. If he were to do so to mine, I don't know for certain that I should send him away. I can't be sure.

ELIZA: Are you satisfied, Deborah, you found a safe messenger for my note?

DEBORAH: O, I made sure of that. Bring me an answer, says I, or bring the company along with you, and I'll give you half a crown. That's the only way, my dear young lady; for as to trusting to their promises – lord! what's a man's promise? I'll go and see if he's coming.

Exit.

ELIZA: What an interview am I awaiting! A Father, – A Mother – what sacred ties! Even though my memory scarcely retains their figures, my heart acknowledges their rights, and palpitates with impatience to shew its instinctive duty.

WAITER: *(Outside.)* Not there, sir, not there! –

ELIZA: Ah! they are come – Joy, now, takes place of all else! *(Hastily opens he door.)* Yes, here! here! here!

WAITER: Very well, meme. O ho, is it so!

LORD JOHN DERVIS and FRANK CLEVELAND present themselves.

They look ELIZA up and down approvingly.

FRANK: Your servant, ma'am.

LORD JOHN: How dost do, Child?

ELIZA: Good Heaven!

FRANK: I am happy in the honour of your commands. What a pretty young thing, my Lord.

LORD JOHN: Consumed pretty.

ELIZA: What a cruel mistake! – I thought – I expected –

FRANK: No excuses, my dear. An adventure may save me from hanging or drowning. O Lord John! if you knew the diabolic run of ill luck I have had! – Not been in bed all night!

LORD JOHN: O the plague!

ELIZA: Gentlemen, I hope – I beg – this apartment –

FRANK: She is immensely handsome.

LORD JOHN: Devilish handsome!

ELIZA: If you will not relinquish my room, suffer me at least to pass to some other.

FRANK: Any other you please. Whither shall I conduct you?

ELIZA: *(Retreating.)* Gentlemen I insist – I – Deborah! – Waiters! – Deborah! –

Enter DEBORAH.

DEBORAH: Hey day, what's this? What's your business here, Misters?

FRANK: What is yours for the enquiry Mrs. Notable?

ELIZA: Do not answer Deborah; but desire somebody to shew me instantly to another apartment.

DEBORAH: That I will, I warrant. Here, Waiter! Waiter!

FRANK: Nay, fair lady, if we are seriously in your way –
Mighty odd this Lord John. What did she call us in for?

LORD JOHN: Confounded odd.

Enter WAITER.

WAITER: Commands?

ELIZA: Be so good, sir, as to let me have some room to myself till the arrival of my friends.

WAITER: Here's one here, meme.

ELIZA: Are you sure I shall be unmolested, there, sir, for the few minutes I have to remain?

WAITER: O yes, meme.

ELIZA: Come then, Deborah.

DEBORAH: Yes my dear young lady.

ELIZA goes into the next room; but as DEBORAH is following, FRANK twitches her back by the arm.

DEBORAH: O lord! you fright me to death! save me, Mr. Waiter, save me!

WAITER: He! He! He!

Exit.

LORD JOHN and FRANK draw DEBORAH from the door.

LORD JOHN: Come, no airs, you old cat.

DEBORAH: Old cat? O!

FRANK: Nay, nay, don't be affronted, my dear, 'tis only a phrase of his Lordship's to his particular favourites. Pray who is that young thing?

DEBORAH: I won't tell you: so let me go.

FRANK: Why then I suppose you don't know, my Angel?

DEBORAH: Not know? Why who went with her to the East Indies then? And who came back with her?

FRANK: East Indies? Has she been to the East Indies?

LORD JOHN: What the plague did she do in the East Indies?

DEBORAH: That's more than the old cat will tell, I promise you.

FRANK: Nay, nay, don't bear malice. You look the very picture of sweetness and gentleness.

DEBORAH: Nay, as to that, I never was reckoned wanting in affability. Though I've met with but base returns, often enough!

FRANK: But perhaps you never heard any of her private history?

DEBORAH: Never heard? Why was not I Housekeeper to Mr. Alderson from the time he adopted her? Did not I buy all the fine things he ordered for her when he took the maggot to make her his heiress? And did not I carry back all her old clothes for her sister, because the family then was as poor as Job? Never heard, indeed!

FRANK: Heiress? What, is she an Heiress? I hope we have not been impertinent. That waiter deserves to have his bones broke for not telling us.

LORD JOHN: O the Deuce! toss him in a blanket.

FRANK: So she's to have a pretty considerable fortune, is she?

DEBORAH: What do you call pretty considerable? She has eighty thousand pounds if she has a penny.

FRANK: Eighty thousand pounds!

LORD JOHN: O the plague! I'll horsepond that waiter in five minutes!

FRANK: And when is this to come into possession?

DEBORAH: As to the when, why it's all in her own hands at this very minute.

FRANK: All her's now? But then, I conclude those poor relations –

DEBORAH: I believe you'd be pretty glad to be half as rich. Why they are like so many Crecusses now.

FRANK: Are they so, faith? – And their names – O, I recollect, their names – ay, their names are Stevens?

DEBORAH: Stevens? You know much of the matter to be sure. Why their names are Watts. He was nothing but an errand boy, or such like, at his beginning. And as to she he married, she was no more than his master's housemaid: a poor mean thing –

ELIZA: *(Within.)* Deborah! Deborah!

DEBORAH: My young lady calls!

FRANK: Deborah?

DEBORAH: Now I wish you were both at old Nick for keeping me so!

Exit.

FRANK: Eighty thousand pounds, my dear Lord John!

LORD JOHN: That waiter deserves the bastinado.

FRANK: Eighty thousand pounds!

LORD JOHN: What the D–l can she do here?

FRANK: Eighty thousand pounds!

LORD JOHN: What? Hast a fancy to 'em?

FRANK: 'Twould be convenient.

LORD JOHN: What, marry? O the plague!

FRANK: The very D–l! And yet, eighty thousand pounds! 'twould be rather convenient.

LORD JOHN: Deuced convenient.

FRANK: And one might have her without much trouble. She can have seen nobody yet. She can know nothing. And I hate trouble.

LORD JOHN: So do I, confoundedly.

FRANK: It's worth a thought. What can I do to scrape acquaintance with her?

LORD JOHN: Horse-whip the waiter.

FRANK: What will that do?

LORD JOHN: Make him call to her to beg him off.

FRANK: Admirable! Here, Waiter! Waiter!

LORD JOHN: Waiter Waiter!

Enter WAITER.

WAITER: Coming, sir.

FRANK: Sir, how came you –

LORD JOHN: Yes, how came you –

WAITER: Here's a coachfull of company enquiring for the young lady.

FRANK: Ha? Let's find out what they are.

LORD JOHN: Yes; but bastinado the waiter: Don't forget that.

FRANK: I will. How came you, I say, –

Enter MR WATTS.

MR WATTS: Where's my Darter?

FRANK: Umph! Pray may I presume, sir, – Are you a relation of the young lady?

MR WATTS: Yes, sir. She's one of my Darters. I've two. T'other's coming upstairs.

FRANK: I believe then, sir, the excessive incompetence of this waiter has obliged the young lady to take refuge in another room.

WAITER: Pretty well for assurance that! That's just such a gentleman as I should like to be myself. *(Apart as he is ejected.)*

FRANK: Will you give me leave, sir, to make use of your name in acquainting the young lady she may return in safety?

MR WATTS: Sir, I shall take it kind. I don't know what she should go pottering a'ter, just as we're all come.

FRANK: Madam! Miss Watts! permit me, I entreat, the honour of offering some apology, and of informing you that Mr Watts in now here.

ELIZA: O where? Where? My Father! my dear Father! *(Drops upon one knee to him.)*

MR WATTS: How do do, my dear? You're welcome home again. Well! I should never have known you! But what have you been a'ter? I hope the waiter ha'nt been sarcy?

Enter MISS WATTS.

MISS WATTS: La, Pa', what did you leave us for so? We've been up the wrong stairs; and I dare say Ma'll be blundering on this half hour.

MR WATTS: Why, my dear, I wanted to see your sister of the soonest, so I e'en put my best foot foremost.

ELIZA: My Sister!

MISS WATTS: O dear, is it you, Sister Eliziana? How you're grown! How do do, Sister? What a pretty hat you've got on! I'll have just the fellow to it. Pray who are those two smart beaus you've got with you?

FRANK: *(Apart to LORD JOHN.)* What a vulgar tribe!

LORD JOHN: Consumed vulgar!

Enter MRS WATTS.

MRS WATTS: Well, I've found my way at last. But I can't think, Tommy, how you could be so rude as to go on at sich a rate, leaving one all alone so. And the stairs are all dirty! Here's all my nice petticoats –

MR WATTS: Why, my dear, I thought your Darter would think it long till she saw us, so I thought –

ELIZA: Is that my Mother? – my dear Mother! –

Runs to MRS WATTS.

MRS WATTS: Take care, my dear, take a little care, or you'll squeeze my poor new Handkerchief till it won't be fit to be seen. And it cost me sich a sight of money –

MISS WATTS: La, Ma', what signifies? I hope you can buy another. *(Whispers her.)* What do you talk so mean for before those two smart gentlemen?

MRS WATTS: Nay, my dear, I don't do it to find fault, for I think it very pretty of your sister to be in sich a hurry; only there's no need to spoil one's things. Come, my dear Betsey –

MISS WATTS: *(Whispering.)* La, Ma', what do you call her Betsey for? you're as bad as Pa'! You know I told you she's to be called Eliziana now.

MRS WATTS: Yes, Elizinana I mean. I'm sure, my dear, I'm very glad to see you again. You've been a long ways. Why you're grown quite a woman my dear!

FRANK: *(Apart to LORD JOHN.)* This won't do Lord John!

LORD JOHN: O confound it, no!

MR WATTS: I wonder why those two fine chaps can't as well go and find out another room! Pray, my dear Darter, what was it took old Alderson off? Did he leave you much over your fourscore? What do you cry for, my dear?

MRS WATTS: I hope you a'n't sorry to see us, my dear?

ELIZA: O no! – but the rememberance of Mr Alderson – his virtues – his benevolence, his unceasing kindness – *(Weeps.)*

MRS WATTS: Pray, my dear, have you got over much Indy muslin? I ha'n't bought a morsel since I knew you was coming.

ELIZA: You will permit me, I hope, to lay all my stores at your feet.

MRS WATTS: I'm sure that's a very pretty thought of you, my dear.

FRANK: *(Apart to LORD JOHN.)* If she i'n't seized quickly, she won't be worth capture.

MRS WATTS: Pray, my dear, who are these two young gentlemen with you?

FRANK: *(Advancing.)* I – I – I –

MR WATTS: Did they travel over in the same ship with you, my dear?

MISS WATTS: La, Pa', I wish you wouldn't talk. The gentleman's going to speak himself.

ELIZA: They are entirely strangers to me, sir.

FRANK: I beg a million of pardons – but I have only waited for a moment's opportunity to express my concern and confusion, and – and – I beg an hundred thousand pardons – I am so utterly confounded – the accident – but the waiter –

LORD JOHN: O the rascal! come and let's murder him.

MISS WATTS: O la!

MRS WATTS: O dear!

FRANK: Don't be alarmed, ladies. We'll step into the next room before we proceed to action. It won't do, Lord John! it won't do!

Apart to LORD JOHN, and exeunt together into the inner room.

MISS WATTS: La, Pa', why didn't you ask 'em to stay? You're always so monstrous stupid!

MRS WATTS: Yes, indeed, Tommy, you're always very stupid: I must say that for you.

MISS WATTS: Pray, Sister Eliziana, where did you get that pretty travelling dress?

ELIZA: It was made in Calcutta.

MISS WATTS: La! can they make things there? I thought they'd been all savages.

MR WATTS: Yes, yes, they can make pretty good things there, I promise you! I suppose there's more hundred thousands made in Calcutta than in all the known world besides.

MISS WATTS: Pray, Sister, do the Indins do much mischief?

ELIZA: Mischief?

MISS WATTS: What kind of look have they? Do they let 'em run about wild? Wa'n't you monstrous frightened at first?

ELIZA: Frightened? The native Gentoos are the mildest and gentlest of human beings.

MISS WATTS: I'm sure I should do nothing but squeal if I was among 'em.

MR WATTS: There's no need for you to go among 'em now, my dear, for I can give you a handsome I war'nt me, as Mr Alderson gave your Sister.

MRS WATTS: It's surprising, my dear Darter Elizeneny, that you didn't get a rich husband yourself there: for I'm told the men in Indy all want wives.

MR WATTS: I'm sure I wish we could send 'em some. I'd spare 'em mine! *(Half aside.)*

MRS WATTS: What's that you say Tommy?

Enter MR TIBBS.

MR TIBBS: I beg pardon, ladies and gentlemen – I was told there was one Mr Watts here. I'm sure I don't know how the waiter could make such a mistake. I beg pardon – *(Bowing frequently and retreating.)*

MR WATTS: Mr Watts? Why pray what do you want with – Oddso! if it i'n't Cousin Joel Tibbs!

MR TIBBS: Why what's it you my dear Tom! Good lauk! I can't believe my eyes!

MR WATTS: My dear Joel Tibbs! *(They embrace.)*

MISS WATTS: La, how provoking Pa' is as if he couldn't have walked off, and made believe he did not know him!

MRS WATTS: Dear if it in't Joel Tibbs. Come, my dears, let's move away.

MR TIBBS: Why how you be decked out! Why I shouldn't have known you if I'd met you anywhere upon the face of Earth.

MR WATTS: My dear Joel, why I ha'n't seen you these eighteen years!

MR TIBBS: Silk stockings, as I live! – And a ruffled shirt! well, if anybody'd have said to me That's Tom Watts, I'd have contradicted 'em as flat as a pancake! And how does Cousin Aylce do?

MR WATTS: Why there she is! why, my dear! why don't you see Cousin Tibbs?

MR TIBBS: What that? Is that Cousin Aylce? Lauk a Day! why the World's turned topsy turvy! Cousin Aylce in a silk gown! And pray what's become of the children? How does Peg do? And little Eliza, that was just beginning to prittle-prattle?

MR WATTS: Why that's Peg! Only think of your not knowing her! Peggy, my dear, turn about and shew yourself. Here's your old Cousin Joel Tibbs.

MISS WATTS: La, Pa', why can't you hold your tongue? What do you call me Peg for? How often have I told you I'm Margarella?

MR TIBBS: What's that Cousin Peg! Good lauk! who'd have thought it! Dressed out like a fine lady in the front boxes! And this must be little Eliza! well, I'm glad the World goes so merrily with you all. But what, don't you know me, Cousin Aylce?

MRS WATTS: Why indeed, as to that, – I can't pretend to say I remember everybody I see.

MR TIBBS: Why then we're even: for I should no more have known you than the Pope. You're prodigious altered. Your eyes – that used to be so sparkish, – why they're as dull! And there's ever such a heap of little wizen wrinkles round 'em.

MRS WATTS: Dear sir, I wish you'd please to look at home! You've not stood still, no more than your neighbours. Come let's go. Tommy! my dear, come, too. What do you stop for?

Exit.

MR WATTS: Well, Girls, do you at least –

MISS WATTS: La, Pa', what do you say Girls for? Can't you
say young ladies? I really think Pa' grows worse and worse
every day. He'll never be the gentleman.

Exit muttering.

ELIZA: Alas! alas! Cleveland! How will he endure an
intercourse so new to him!

Apart and exit.

MR TIBBS: Well, I declare! who'd have thought of their
flouncing off so! Do you think, Cousin, Aylce minded
about her eyes? I said it for no harm.

MR WATTS: Ah! my dear Joel Tibbs! I've a deal to tell you of
our new ways!

MR TIBBS: How lucky it was I should happen to go by just
now! I was thinking of you no more than the post; but I
saw a shay broke down, as I was walking along, so I stopt
to ask who it belonged to; and they thought I asked whose
the coach was – Good lauk, Tom, that ever I should live
to see you keep your coach! Such a poor snivelling Boy
as I remember you! – Well, they said 'twas 'squire Watts's.
Watts? – says I; why sure –

Exit talking. Re-enter LORD JOHN, and FRANK.

FRANK: What's to be done, my dear Lord John? What's to be
done in this desperate moment?

LORD JOHN: O the very D–l of a moment!

FRANK: These people are so extravagantly vulgar –

LORD JOHN: O, confound it! don't think of them.

FRANK: Though it would not much signify, I should never see
them, after the horrid bore of the ceremony. But then, –
my aunt – Lady Wilhelmina – she'd never forgive it. Such
a set of new Nephews and Neices and Cousins – I don't
know if it would not cost her an apoplectic fit.

LORD JOHN: O the plague! Give it up.

FRANK: And yet my dear lord – 'tis a barbarous temptation – she seems thrown into my very hands – and…I have not at this moment a guinea left in the World!

LORD JOHN: Not a guinea?

FRANK: Not a crown, by Jupiter!

LORD JOHN: Not a crown?

FRANK: Not a sixpence; by Mars, Jupiter, and Apollo!

LORD JOHN: O take her, then, take her! 'Tis better than the King's Bench.

FRANK: And she is really young and pretty. – 'Twould be but a charity. I must positively think of it. A little rhodomontade is all she can require. Come, my Lord John, you can help me. You shall go and tell Sir Marmaduke and my Aunt Wilhelmina that 'tis my fixt resolve to take this measure: and then, either they will draw their purse strings and pay my debts, or I'll fairly put the eighty thousand pounds into my pocket.

ACT II

Later that morning. A drawing room at SIR MARMADUKE TYLNEY'S
SIR MARMADUKE *is reading his newspaper. Enter* MISS CLEVELAND
running.

MISS CLEVELAND: Sir Marmaduke! Sir Marmaduke! ill news!
Robert is just returned from Tylney Hall, and he says –

SIR MARMADUKE: Why, what's the matter now? Are any of
my tenants run away?

MISS CLEVELAND: No, but there broke out such a dreadful
fire in the village yesterday morning –

SIR MARMADUKE: You don't say so? Has it done any mischief
to Tylney Hall?

MISS CLEVELAND: No, Sir Marmaduke, not to Tylney Hall;
but –

SIR MARMADUKE: Why then, what do you put on such a long
face for? I hate a long face for nothing. Would you have
just that single village in the whole World, exempt from
mischief, lest that blockhead Robert should be frightened?

MISS CLEVELAND: No, but there are so many sufferers! –

SIR MARMADUKE: Well, don't make such a pother if there are.
Everybody must submit to accident.

MISS CLEVELAND: Poor old Mr Walters threw himself from
his chamber window, and broke both his legs.

SIR MARMADUKE: Well, well, well, who can help it? What's
the use of repining? I hate repining.

MISS CLEVELAND: And Lord Garman has had a narrow
escape. A flake of fire fell upon his head just as he was
getting into his carriage, and one whole side of his Hair has
been singed off.

SIR MARMADUKE: A mighty matter, truly! as if his barber
could not furnish him with another. Learn to make light

of little evils, Niece. If every trifling misfortune is to be aggravated in this manner –

MISS CLEVELAND: And another flake lighted upon our little Hay-rick near the Barn, and burnt it to the ground.

SIR MARMADUKE: What, what do you say?

MISS CLEVELAND: A flake of fire lighted upon our little Hayrick, and consumed it in a minute.

SIR MARMADUKE: The D–l it did?

MISS CLEVELAND: Yes, Sir Marmaduke; but it's only the little one.

SIR MARMADUKE: Only? Only? There is not a thing I had a more particular value for. I had rather by half the whole village had been burnt!

MISS CLEVELAND: The great stack appears quite safe; and we have fared better than anybody else in all the neighbourhood, for Squire Pollard and Squire Milton have lost –

SIR MARMADUKE: And pray what do I care for them? My little Hay-rick! – There was never so unfortunate a thing since the World was formed! This year, too, of all others – My little Hay-rick! – *(Exit.)*

Enter LADY WILHELMINA TYLNEY.

MISS CLEVELAND: O Lady Wilhelmina! have you heard of this terrible fire that Robert brings the account of from Tylney Hall?

LADY WILHELMINA: Yes. It has extremely affected me. I find Lord Garman has nearly lost all his Hair.

MISS CLEVELAND: O, that's nothing! but poor old Walters has broken both his legs!

LADY WILHELMINA: Nothing, Miss Cleveland? I am surprised to hear you speak so lightly of a misfortune of that nature to such a Nobleman as Lord Garman, whose Hair was so deservedly admired. As to old – what is it the man calls himself? – persons of his class must naturally expect to be exposed, now and then, to some disagreeable events.

MISS CLEVELAND: Dear madam, does not your La'ship think it a greater evil for a poor man to lose his legs, than for a man of rank to lose his Hair?

LADY WILHELMINA: Certainly not. A man of rank is peculiarly susceptible to evil, because not brought up to vulgar vicissitudes; but a low person has so little leisure to reflect or refine, that a few disagreeable accidents can make but little impression upon him.

MISS CLEVELAND: Ah Lady Wilhelmina! – Pardon me – but because you do not enquire into the poor man's feelings, is it therefore to be concluded he has none?

LADY WILHELMINA: That is a point I do not investigate. And, indeed, Miss Cleveland, if you discoursed rather more rarely of people of that description yourself, I should think it more becoming a young woman of fashion. As to me, I confess I always feel degraded for the rest of the day, when I have been induced to converse upon any low subjects.

MISS CLEVELAND: May I beg your La'ship's permission for the carriage to call upon Miss Percival?

LADY WILHELMINA: Willingly. That is an acquaintance you cannot too much cultivate. I always encouraged it, even before the death of her noble Brother, and our views of affinity.

Enter LORD JOHN unannounced.

LORD JOHN: Servant, good folks. Hope you're all well. What a confounded morning.

LADY WILHELMINA: Lord John! I feared the Porter had admitted someone not upon my list.

LORD JOHN: How so, Lady Wil?

LADY WILHELMINA: The mode of your entry is so entirely new to me, Lord John, that it might have led me to apprehend one of your Lordship's grooms – you'll pardon me, my Lord – had taken the liberty to present himself before me in person.

LORD JOHN: What kept you from the Coffee Room last night?

MISS CLEVELAND: I was not at the Opera.

LORD JOHN: No? What in the World did you do with yourself?

MISS CLEVELAND: I was preparing for the return of my Brother. We may now reasonably hope to see him in a day or two. The wind has been so delightfully fair –

Enter SIR MARMADUKE in riding clothes.

SIR MARMADUKE: Fair? And be hanged to it! It was so rough and harsh yesterday, it cut me off from my ride.

MISS CLEVELAND: But if it facilitates his return, after a voyage so long, so dangerous, so painful –

SIR MARMADUKE: Pish! What's his voyage to my ride?

MISS CLEVELAND: I thought you were quite anxious to see him?

SIR MARMADUKE: Well, so I am: but there's no need I should lose my ride to hurry him home.

MISS CLEVELAND: O shocking!

SIR MARMADUKE: Pho, pho, don't make such a fuss about nothing. You know I can't bear to lose my ride. And what harm can it do a young man to be a week or two more or less in a warm comfortable Cabin?

LORD JOHN: Sir Marmaduke, may I speak to you upon a little business?

SIR MARMADUKE: I never meddle with other people's affairs. *(Going.)*

LORD JOHN: O but this is an affair of your own.

SIR MARMADUKE: An affair of my own? *(Turning short back.)*

LORD JOHN: Yes; that is of your Nephew, my friend Frank Cleveland.

SIR MARMADUKE: What, he wants money, again, I suppose?

LORD JOHN: Plaguely.

SIR MARMADUKE: I thought so. Your servant, my Lord.

Exit.

LORD JOHN: O the D–l! I'll open the case to you then, Lady Wil.

LADY WILHELMINA: I am always happy to converse with your Lordship; but as to Mr Francis Cleveland's affairs, I make it a point never to interfere in them. *(Going.)*

LORD JOHN: Poor Frank! then he must e'en marry the little Cockney!

LADY WILHELMINA: *(Returning.)* My Lord?

MISS CLEVELAND: Lord John!

LORD JOHN: Why it's a horrid bore; but what's to be done? A man must eat and drink.

MISS CLEVELAND: But what is it you mean, Lord John?

LORD JOHN: That he has just met with a nice little Cit, who dies to have a woman of quality for her aunt.

LADY WILHELMINA: Lord John, permit me to say, you allow yourself to associate with persons beneath your dignity, till you acquire habits of familiarity that have rather an unpleasant effect.

MISS CLEVELAND: Do pray, Lord John, explain yourself. Has my brother Frank really had the good sense and the good fortune to form a connexion with any respectable family in the City?

LADY WILHELMINA: Miss Cleveland?

LORD JOHN: Respectable Family? Why they are as much below the City as us! The vulgarest tribe!

MISS CLEVELAND: O fie, fie Frank!

LADY WILHELMINA: And is it possible, is it credible, Lord John, you can condescend to bear us such an embassy?

LORD JOHN: Why what the plague can a poor fellow do Lady Wil? He can't starve.

LADY WILHELMINA: And can you, my Lord, think mixing with persons of such a stamp –

LORD JOHN: Better than starving? Yes, I can faith.

LADY WILHELMINA: Intolerable! this must be put an end to. Lord John, assure him of our highest displeasure.

LORD JOHN: May I assure him you'll pay his debts?

LADY WILHELMINA: Impossible! we are just engaged in forming an establishment for his elder brother. But tell him we will make every exertion in his favour. Tell him I will myself intercede for sending him to the East Indies in his Brother's place.

LORD JOHN: What to fag? O the plague! no, no, Lady Wil! you won't catch Frank at fagging.

Enter CLEVELAND.

CLEVELAND: Lady Wilhelmina.

MISS CLEVELAND: *(Running to embrace him.)* My dear Brother!

CLEVELAND: My dearest Sister!

LADY WILHELMINA: I am so much disconcerted, I can scarcely speak. Mr Cleveland, give me leave to congratulate you upon your safe return.

CLEVELAND: Your Ladyship is extremely good. I hope my Uncle –

Enter SIR MARMADUKE.

SIR MARMADUKE: My dear Nephew!

CLEVELAND: I have obeyed your summons, sir, with all the promptitude in my power.

SIR MARMADUKE: And you shall be well rewarded. I have not sent for you over upon a fool's errand. Give me credit for that. I think at last *(In a low voice.)* I have got a handsome provision for you.

LADY WILHELMINA: If you wish to speak with Mr Cleveland alone, Sir Marmaduke, my Lord John will favour Miss Cleveland and me with his company in my dressing room.

I can hardly breathe! To be connected with persons of such a class!

Exit.

MISS CLEVELAND: My dear Brother! *(Shakes hands with CLEVELAND and follows.)*

LORD JOHN: I've put her in the D–l of a worry.

Exit.

SIR MARMADUKE: Well, my dear Nephew, and what now, do you think has made me send for you back?

CLEVELAND: I wait your own time for information, sir.

SIR MARMADUKE: What will you take for your voyage?

CLEVELAND: Your kindness, sir.

SIR MARMADUKE: Ay, ay; but how much will satisfy you?

CLEVELAND: Sir, I, – I –

SIR MARMADUKE: Come, what will do? Be honest.

CLEVELAND: Sir, I have not formed the smallest –

SIR MARMADUKE: Well, what say you to ten thousand pounds?

CLEVELAND: My dear Uncle!

SIR MARMADUKE: Come, speak; what say you to it?

CLEVELAND: You confound me, Sir Marmaduke! Munificence such as this –

SIR MARMADUKE: Well, if that flutters you, skip over to another five.

CLEVELAND: Sir?

SIR MARMADUKE: Skip over to another five I say, and tell me what you have to object to fifteen thousand pounds.

CLEVELAND: O Sir Marmaduke! you distress, you overpower me!

SIR MARMADUKE: Well then, will you come to yourself if I say twenty thousand?

CLEVELAND: Sir!

SIR MARMADUKE: Will that bring you to yourself, I say?

CLEVELAND: Are you laughing at me?

SIR MARMADUKE: No.

CLEVELAND: You mean then, – you allude – I fancy, I now comprehend your generous though melancholy purpose.

SIR MARMADUKE: Melancholy? No. What is there melancholy in twenty thousand pounds? However if you think it so shocking, will it relieve you to double it?

CLEVELAND: Double it?

SIR MARMADUKE: Nay, then, treble it at once. And there ends my lesson of Arithmetic for this morning. Sixty thousand pounds.

CLEVELAND: My dear Uncle, I am totally at a loss to comprehend you. My perplexity encreases every moment.

SIR MARMADUKE: There is only one condition annexed to it. You are to marry for it.

CLEVELAND: Marry?

SIR MARMADUKE: Yes, to take to you a wife. How you stare! Why, I am not going to propose to you an old Hag, like – *(In a low voice.)* your poor Aunt, God help me! Are you sure that door i'n't ajar?

CLEVELAND: Relieve me from this suspense, I conjure you, sir!

SIR MARMADUKE: Why it's to Miss – O you young rascal! What a happy thing it is to be a young rascal! – It's to Miss Percival.

CLEVELAND: Miss Percival?

SIR MARMADUKE: Yes. That pretty little frisky thing, Miss Percival. She has been violently in love with you these two years. We all saw that she had a hankering after you; but as she had next to nothing, we never noticed it. However you were hardly sailed, when her rich brother, Lord Percival, departed, and left her all he had at his own disposal. Well! Why don't you jump?

CLEVELAND: I am in such amazement –

SIR MARMADUKE: As soon as she came into possession, she whispered her secret to your sister; and your sister whispered it to your Aunt; and your Aunt whispered it to me; and I suppose by this time, it is whispered into half a dozen news-papers. Jemima asked her leave to write for you over. She was too skittish to consent; but she did not say nay; only she insisted I should take the recalling you upon myself. Why don't you jump, I say?

CLEVELAND: I am so astonished, so confounded, so disturbed –

SIR MARMADUKE: Yes, yes, you are badly off! well, not to be wanting on our side, upon so splendid an occasion, I agreed to make over to you my Lincolnshire Estate immediately. –

CLEVELAND: O Uncle! and upon these terms only must I hope –

SIR MARMADUKE: No, no; I made my own terms. I demanded ready money, in return, to buy off my mortgage. To this she consented; and therefore you have now only to take her fair hand. So off with your boots, and your travelling dress, and throw yourself at her feet.

CLEVELAND: Hear me first, my dear Uncle, and suffer my little narrative to meet with your indulgence. On my arrival at Calcutta –

Enter MISS CLEVELAND.

MISS CLEVELAND: Lady Wilhelmina begs to know, Uncle, if you will see Lord John before he goes, and hear from himself his very alarming account of Frank?

SIR MARMADUKE: Pish! that's no business of mine. Pray leave us alone.

Enter LADY WILHELMINA.

LADY WILHELMINA: There was no detaining Lord John, Sir Marmaduke, while you hesitated whether to admit him. My good Cleveland, how opportune is your return at this distressing juncture! you know nothing, I imagine of this dishonouring plan of your graceless Brother?

CLEVELAND: Of Frank?

LADY WILHELMINA: O the most preposterous conduct! He is determined upon disgracing us all, by an ignominious alliance with a young woman out of the City!

CLEVELAND: The City? Confusion! *(Walking away.)*

LADY WILHELMINA: Your start satisfies me; you feel the indignity like myself.

CLEVELAND: Indeed, madam, – on the contrary –

LADY WILHELMINA: Spare yourself the violence of attempting to excuse him. The disorder into which you are thrown explains to me your real sentiments.

CLEVELAND: I protest, Lady Wilhelmina, –

SIR MARMADUKE: Is the girl rich?

LADY WILHELMINA: People of that sort commonly are; but I did not judge it necessary to enquire. I believe Miss Cleveland might hear what was said upon that subject.

MISS CLEVELAND: Yes, Uncle, she has a very large fortune.

SIR MARMADUKE: Why then where's the harm of Frank's entertaining it at his Banker's?

LADY WILHELMINA: The harm, Sir Marmaduke? The harm of mingling with people of that description? The very lowest, Lord John says, –

SIR MARMADUKE: Well, what's that to us? Who cares about the genealogy of a younger brother's wife? If it were my Nephew Cleveland, indeed, who may become the head of this house –

CLEVELAND: Distraction! *(Apart.)*

LADY WILHELMINA: Cleveland, I exult in your honourable agitation. Let me see you in my dressing room, that we may deliberate what steps to take to preserve our family pure from an alliance with a native of the City.

Exit.

SIR MARMADUKE: Pho, pho, Cleveland, don't look so confounded. Make yourself up for paying your devoirs to Miss Percival, and leave Frank to his devices. If he can once manage his affairs, and pay his debts by himself, I shall never ask if his Banker lives at Cornhill or St James'. What difference does it make to me?

Exit.

MISS CLEVELAND: I confess myself utterly astonished my dear Brother, at your altered sentiments. How often have I heard you declare, that you knew many characters as well informed, as well educated, and as amiable in the City as at our end of the Town? Why so readily have you joined with Lady Wilhelmina in contemning poor Frank?

CLEVELAND: My dearest Jemima, I have been wholly misconceived by Lady Wilhelmina, and the surprise and confusion – robbed me of presence of mind to rectify her mistake – O Jemima! within that City – was born the beloved object of every hope of my heart!

MISS CLEVELAND: Is it possible? Frank, then, is more than justified – but alas for poor Miss Percival! – your affections are engaged?

CLEVELAND: Why Miss Percival has honoured me with her choice I cannot tell: certainly not from any interchange of partiality; for though she is gay and agreeable, and I have taken pleasure in rallying and chatting with her, she is vain and fantastic and …

FRANK: *(Within.)* Where is he?

MISS CLEVELAND: I hear the voice of Frank.

CLEVELAND: Leave us together a few minutes, my dear Jemima, and we may concur in forming some mutual plan to subdue the prejudices of Lady Wilhelmina.

MISS CLEVELAND: That will be a conquest indeed, for they are as wide from reason as from feeling.

Exit.

CLEVELAND: O my lovely Eliza! how shall I claim you of your Friends, without the inheritance of which I thought myself so secure!

Enter FRANK.

FRANK: Brother, your hand! most heartily welcome back to England.

CLEVELAND: I rejoice to see you again, my dear Frank.

FRANK: Fair wind, fair fortune, and a fair lady have wafted you home most prosperously. I congratulate you upon them with all my heart, and that without spite or envy; though a more pitiable contrast to such enjoyments never yet was offered by living wight than by your most obsequious servant.

CLEVELAND: Inform me how you are circumstanced, dear Frank, and accept my best services.

FRANK: You will feel, I know, for my distress; but have a care you do not draw back when you hear of my resource!

CLEVELAND: Fear me not. I am under much present embarrassment myself, and reciprocal confidence may lead to reciprocal relief. Speak without reserve.

FRANK: I have been so inhumanly hard run, that I am compelled, at length, to consent to the most horrid of sacrifices.

CLEVELAND: How so?

FRANK: Faith, I am ashamed to say.

CLEVELAND: No; no; trust me.

FRANK: 'Tis a violent measure; you'll never believe it.

CLEVELAND: Why not?

FRANK: I must marry.

CLEVELAND: Marry?

FRANK: Nothing less.

CLEVELAND: And who is the honoured object at whose shrine you are to be thus offered?

FRANK: Why that, Brother, is the D–l of the business. I must take up with – now don't despise me, – a Cit!

CLEVELAND: Despise you, my dear Frank? On the contrary. You know that I – that the City – but what is the lady's name?

FRANK: Why there again, I suppose you will all fly out. However, that, you know, she will change. Meanwhile, 'tis short at least. What do you think of Watts?

CLEVELAND: Watts?

FRANK: Nay, don't jump so! 'Tis not in Lady Wilhelmina's Herald's office, I grant; but still –

CLEVELAND: Hold, hold! – Has this lady a Sister?

FRANK: O yes; and a Father and a Mother, – and half a hundred Cousins and Uncles, and Aunts and Grandmothers.

CLEVELAND: Where does she live?

FRANK: In Bond Street.

CLEVELAND: In Bond Street? Nay then, my dear Frank she is probably –

FRANK: I must not deceive you, though; for, to own the truth, she is but just disembarked from the East Indies.

CLEVELAND: The East Indies?

FRANK: Why you jump higher and higher! Perhaps you knew her there?

CLEVELAND: From what part of the East Indies does she come?

FRANK: From the land of the Hottentots for aught I can tell. I never enquired, But hold! Perhaps you may have heard of her; for I now recollect gathering that her residence had been at Calcutta.

CLEVELAND: Calcutta!

FRANK: You start like a Ghost in a Tragedy! I hope you know no harm of her?

CLEVELAND: If you mean this for raillery, sir, give me leave to tell you 'tis the worst-timed, and most unfeeling –

FRANK: Raillery? I have not such a thought. But if I had, – must I turn Methodist Preacher, because, while you pay your addresses to a fair honourable, I am reduced to taking up with a little City Gentoo?

CLEVELAND: A City Gentoo? Frank, this is an excess of levity that I find wholly beyond endurance. You will please to have done with it. And never let me hear that lady's name from you again.

FRANK: And why not? What are you so fierce? 'Tis a pretty little name enough, I think, and too glib to the tongue to be very fatiguing to the ear. However, if it enrages you so, I must be the quicker in making her change it.

CLEVELAND: Frank –

FRANK: Really, Brother, though I expected to put Lady Wilhelmina in flames, I was by no means prepared to see you thus irritated at my taking a rib out of the City.

CLEVELAND: I irritated at a connexion with the City? – Tell me, however, did you ever even see this young lady you speak of thus securely and presumptuously? Never; I am certain.

FRANK: Ha! Ha! why it is not an hour since I left her.

CLEVELAND: And where, pray, sir?

FRANK: At a rather awkward place; but 'twas where we chanced to meet. 'Twas at a house belonging to a friend of mine in St James' Street.

CLEVELAND: Impossible!

FRANK: 'Tis my last stake; so I beg you will not think me more a plebian than yourself. It has nothing to do with my taste, I assure you; for I hold a Citizen, and Temple Bar in as sovereign contempt as you can do for the life of you.

CLEVELAND: Insufferable! How dare you, sir –

FRANK: Hey day!

CLEVELAND: How dare you, I say, speak thus disrespectfully of the City? Of the first characters for worth and probity in the kingdom.

FRANK: Hey day! Why then what are you in such a passion about?

CLEVELAND: Characters that are the nation's support by their affluence, and the nation's honour by their integrity?

FRANK: Why then what the Deuce do you object to?

Enter MISS CLEVELAND.

MISS CLEVELAND: What is the matter, my dear Brothers? Why do I hear you so loud?

FRANK: He foams so with pride and fury, he knows not a word he says.

CLEVELAND: My dear Jemima where can I speak with you a few moments alone?

MISS CLEVELAND: I expect the carriage every instant to take me to Miss Percival.

CLEVELAND: You must not see her till I have conversed with you. I must entreat you to wait upon the lady I have mentioned to you, and conjure her, in my name to grant me a five minutes audience immediately. The confusion this hair-brained coxcomb may create in the house by his unintelligible assertions can only be prevented, or cleared away, by an instantaneous meeting. Nor shall I think myself at liberty to declare our connexion, till I have revealed to her the disappointment of my expectations from Sir Marmaduke.

MISS CLEVELAND: But what is her name? And where does she live? And how shall I introduce myself? And whom am I to enquire for?

CLEVELAND: Drive slowly to Kensington Gardens. I will but stop to prepare you a note of introduction and join you at the Gate. In a quarter of an hour's walk we can arrange our proceeding. It will be taken for granted, here, you are gone to Miss Percival.

MISS CLEVELAND: It will make me happy to be of the smallest service to you.

Exit CLEVELAND.

FRANK: I'm heartily glad he's gone. This Indian expedition, Jemima, has actually turned his head with arrogance and vanity. He put himself into such desperate choler while I was talking to him of my little Cit, and took such an antipathy to her poor tiny name, that he ordered me never to pronounce it again; and I thought, once or twice, he would have knocked me down.

Enter LORD JOHN DERVIS.

LORD JOHN: What the plague did you give me the slip for, Frank?

MISS CLEVELAND: For the very reason, probably, I shall now do the same – to get rid of you! *(Aside and exit.)*

FRANK: I wanted to see my Brother. But we make no way here, my dear Lord John!

LORD JOHN: The D–l you don't.

FRANK: No; the house is as full of rage as a man need wish it.

LORD JOHN: The plague it is. Why then e'en take the girl.

FRANK: So I will, if the bait does not require much trouble. But how can I get at her?

LORD JOHN: Send her a ladder of ropes.

FRANK: No, not yet; that must be after the Papa has refused me. One must not break through old established customs. However, as I've all to ask and nothing to offer, the

Papa won't fail to play his part in rejecting me. The only difficulty is how to get into the house. It will demand but little skill how to get out of it.

LORD JOHN: Call and ask them how they do.

FRANK: They'll be all in bed – or out – or dressing – or at dinner. I may be a month without catching them.

LORD JOHN: Write to her, then, and come to the point at once.

FRANK: No. I'll write to her Father, One has no chance with a young Girl till her Family are all against one. Or suppose you should write for me, Lord John?

LORD JOHN: Deuce take me if I do!

FRANK: You can set me off much better than I can myself. Besides a Lord is always identified; but who, on t'other side of Temple Bar, knows anything of Frank Cleveland?

LORD JOHN: O the plague! no, no, no, Frank. Anything but that. I hate writing.

FRANK: Come, my Lord, here's pen, and ink, and paper.

LORD JOHN: Faith not I. I can't abide writing. I hate pedantry.

FRANK: Yes, yes, you must. 'Twill have a most pompous effect upon little Miss to be demanded through a Lord. Come, I'll take no denial – Here, sit down.

LORD JOHN: O the D–l. Write!

FRANK: *(Forcing him to sit, and putting a pen into his hand.)* Yes; say my many amiable qualities have induced you to come forwards, upon this interesting occasion, as guarantee of my honour, and singularly estimable character. Come, say something handsome for me.

LORD JOHN: O confound it! I could not write all that in an hour.

FRANK: Well, then, only say, my very deserving and even meritorious young friend.

LORD JOHN: Stop: stop! not so much at once. *My very deserving and even (Writes.)* What's the other word?

FRANK: Meritorious.

LORD JOHN: What should I write meritorious for?

FRANK: What for? Because it's a fine-sounding word!

LORD JOHN: How the D–l do you spell it? I always forget.

FRANK: I'll put it down for you. There. Now add young friend, Mr Francis Cleveland.

LORD JOHN: O the plague! – how I hate writing! I wish it had never been invented; young what, did you say?

FRANK: Friend; to be sure.

LORD JOHN: Do you spell it with an i, or an e?

FRANK: With both.

LORD JOHN: O the Deuce! I've only put an e; does it signify?

FRANK: Not much. Go on. Why now you've left out Francis.

LORD JOHN: I wish it was all at Jericho, with all my soul! Put it in yourself. I'm plaguy tired.

FRANK: Never mind. 'Twill sound more respectable without the christian name. Now say Nephew to Sir Marmaduke Tylney –

LORD JOHN: Stop stop! Is Nephew writ n.e.v. or n.e.f.? It's the oddest thing in the world, but I never can keep that stupid word in my head.

Enter MISS CLEVELAND.

MISS CLEVELAND: Miss Percival is just come, it is impossible I can refuse seeing her.

FRANK: Let's go to your house then Lord John, and one of your servants can run with it as soon as it is done. Send a good smart fellow.

LORD JOHN: 'Tis a most deuced bore. I never was so consumed tired in my life.

Exeunt at one door, and enter MISS PERCIVAL at another.

MISS PERCIVAL: My dear Jemima, you must come and pass the day with me. I am dying of the vapours. These India ships are certainly all lost.

MISS CLEVELAND: I cannot possibly wait upon you this morning; but in the evening –

MISS PERCIVAL: O I shall be dead before the evening; if you don't come directly. I can only invite you by my executors.

MISS CLEVELAND: I have so particular an engagement –

MISS PERCIVAL: Break it, break it! How can you be so formal?

MISS PERCIVAL: I am in agonies to consult you about my first appearance before a certain horrid wretch of your acquaintance. I mean provided I ever happen to see him again. But don't you think, Jemima, he is certainly drowned?

MISS CLEVELAND: No; Cleveland is …

MISS PERCIVAL: Heavens! Is he arrived? O the Wretch! Let me run away this instant. I would not see him for the Universe. Perfidious Jemima! was this a plot to take me by surprise?

MISS CLEVELAND: No, I assure you; it is only –

MISS PERCIVAL: I can't stay to hear you; I am fluttered to death. I can't possibly see him this half year. (*Going.*) Pray what room does the Wretch inhabit? I am so terribly afraid of meeting him –

MISS CLEVELAND: He is gone out.

MISS PERCIVAL: Gone out? To Piccadilly I suppose? To my house? Well, then, I'll stay here; for I can't possibly receive him. At least not these three months. How does the Monster look?

MISS CLEVELAND: Extremely well.

MISS PERCIVAL: The Miscreant! I'm horribly mad you sent for him over. Ten to one if I like him now. How could I be such a fool? I have been upon the point of listening to twenty others since. He's like a husband already; in the way of everything.

MISS CLEVELAND: If you wish it, my dear Miss Percival, I can undertake to persuade him –

MISS PERCIVAL: O undertake nothing, I beseech you. You must not mind a word I say. Don't you know I doat upon him to distraction? But what do you think he'll do in Piccadilly when he misses me?

MISS CLEVELAND: I believe he is not gone to Piccadilly this morning.

MISS PERCIVAL: Not gone to Piccadilly?

MISS CLEVELAND: He had an appointment, I understood, in Kensington Gardens.

MISS PERCIVAL: An appointment in Kensington Gardens? Vastly well! vastly well! extremely well indeed! I am amazingly glad!

MISS CLEVELAND: Do not be offended, I beg. The appointment, to be sincere was but with me.

MISS PERCIVAL: O it's extremely well. Perhaps, when he has finished all his affairs, and his appointments, and strolled a few hours in Kensington Gardens, he may intend calling in Piccadilly? Do you think he will be so good?

MISS CLEVELAND: If you were not so angry, I might have been tempted to beg the loan of your carriage for a quarter of an hour, after it had set you down in Piccadilly.

MISS PERCIVAL: What, to go to Kensington Gardens? Nay, if the appointment is really with you, and with you only, perhaps it is merely to make some enquiries concerning me? Now do tell me!

MISS CLEVELAND: It is certainly only to meet me.

MISS PERCIVAL: Why then, probably the creature wants to make you bring him to me at once! How could you tell it me in so lifeless a manner? My dear Jemima, you want a shaking prodigiously. Come, I'll carry you to the Garden

Gate myself. I can peep at the Wretch through the back Glass, you know, without being seen. How delightful! don't forget, though, that I positively can't receive him these three weeks.

MISS CLEVELAND: If I had any other means to prevent my poor Brother from waiting in vain, I could not thus abuse your goodness.

MISS PERCIVAL: Come, then, run! fly! how slow you are! Heavens, I wish you were in love, Child! I always think everybody looks fast asleep that isn't in love.

Exeunt.

ACT III

Half an hour later. A sunny day in Kensington Gardens. There are benches and a sundial.

MR WATTS, MRS WATTS, MISS WATTS, and ELIZA are walking together.

MR WATTS: Well, Bet, my dear, what say you to Kinsington Garden?

MISS WATTS: La, Pa', now you're calling her Bet again!

MR WATTS: Well, my dear, don't scold. I can't never remember that new name.

MRS WATTS: Why no more can I, my dear, as to that. Not that I mean to 'scuse your Pa' in the least. Why, my dear, why you look no how? What's the matter? *(To ELIZA.)*

ELIZA: My long voyage has a little fatigued me. Nothing else.

MR WATTS: Why I told you so! bringing her out before a bit of dinner, after crossing all them seas!

MISS WATTS: La, Pa', would you have her be as stupid as you? I'm sure I would not have lost such a day for Kinsington Gardens for never so much.

MRS WATTS: *(To MISS WATTS.)* Dear, my dear, do but look at your gownd! Only see how it trails!

MISS WATTS: La, Ma', I hope I need not be always taking care of my things now!

MR WATTS: Nay, my dear, nobody's by.

MISS WATTS: Yes, but somebody's coming; and a very fine gentleman, too. Only think, now, if he should have heard you! Making one look so mean!

Enter the VALET of LORD JOHN DERVIS.

VALET: Pray, sir, may I take the liberty to ask if you're the gentleman this letter's for?

MR WATTS: *(Reading the Direction.)* – Watts Esquire – Bond Street – Why it may be me and it may not; for here's no

Thomas. Pray, sir, can you tell me if Thomas was the other name that i'n't put down?

VALET: If you are Mr Watts, sir, most likely you are the gentleman; for I'm just come from Mr Watts in Bond Street, and the Porter told me his master was in Kinsington Gardens.

MRS WATTS: Dear, Tommy, why are you so shilly-shally? Let me look at the letter myself.

MISS WATTS: La, Ma', you won't read it in half an hour. Give it to me, Pa'.

MR WATTS: No, my dear, I never shew my letters till I have read 'em, in case of private business. Why if it i'n't a whole half sheet of gilt paper wasted in a kiver! *(Reads to himself.)*

MRS WATTS: Come, let's sit down, young ladies, on this nice seat. Won't you sit down, too, sir? Peggy, my dear, – O Peggerelly I mean –

MISS WATTS: Peggerelly? No, it's Margerella, I tell you!

MRS WATTS: Well, my dear, I mean Margarelly: make a little room for the gentleman.

MISS WATTS: It's a very pleasant day, sir.

VALET: Very much so, ma'am.

MISS WATTS: Pray, sir, have you been long in the Gardens, sir?

VALET: Only a few seconds, ma'am. I was uneasy to put the letter into Mr Watts' own hand, and therefore, missing him at home –

MR WATTS: Well, here's a thing to make one stare if one will or no! Why Bet – Elizenny, my dear, here's a gentleman wants to be coming a courting to you already.

ELIZA: To me, sir?

MISS WATTS: La, Pa', let's see. Are you sure it's to Eliziana?

MRS WATTS: More like it's to Margarelly, Tommy, for who should know of Elizenenny's being here?

MISS WATTS: La, it means me I dare say!

ELIZA: Will you permit me, sir, – Will you – give me leave to see – to ask – by what – name the letter is signed?

MISS WATTS: It's Billy Bond, ten to one. But I'm sure, I won't have him now.

MR WATTS: Why a name I never heard in my days, my dear, one John Dervis.

ELIZA: 'Tis certainly some mistake, then, sir. It cannot mean me. How prompt were my expectations to deceive me! *(Aside.)*

MISS WATTS: Why then it must be me! La, how droll! Why I never heard of John Dervis neither! I wonder where's he's seen me!

MR WATTS: No, it can't mean you, my dear, for here's your Sister's name at full length.

ELIZA: It must be written, then, sir, for some foolish sport. Pray return it unanswered.

MR WATTS: So I will, my dear. Be so kind, sir, to take back this here letter to John Dervis, and tell him –

VALET: Who, sir?

MR WATTS: John Dervis, sir, as wrote me the letter. Tell him my darter says –

VALET: Do you mean my Lord, sir?

MR WATTS: My Lord? Why what do you mean? Here's nothing about a my lord here.

MISS WATTS: La, Pa', perhaps the letter's from a Lord? Pray let me look at it.

MRS WATTS: No, let me see it first Tommy. I never see a letter from a Lord in my life. *(Takes the letter.)*

MR WATTS: Why how can this here John Dervis be a Lord?

VALET: He's the second son of the Marquis of Wistborough.

MISS WATTS: La, Pa', and how rude you've behaved!

ELIZA: Still I suspect some trick or some impertinence, for Lord John Dervis is utterly unknown to me. Will you permit me, madam, to look at the hand?

MRS WATTS: Dear, my dear, why I ha'n't made out hardly two words yet.

MR WATTS: Well, see but how people are upon the catch when one's got a little money! Please to tell his Lordship Lord John Dervis –

MISS WATTS: La, Pa', don't give him the letter till I've looked at it. Why what signifies your holding it, Ma'? You know you can't read writing hand. *(Takes the letter.)*

MRS WATTS: Well, I might have made out some of it: snatching things away so!

MISS WATTS: *(Reads.)* "Sir, My very deserving and even meritorious young frend, Mr Cleveland"

ELIZA: Heavens!

MISS WATTS: "Nephew of Sir Marmaduke Tylney –"

ELIZA: Ah Sister, dear Sister, let me have the letter I conjure you! –

MISS WATTS: "has given me in charge to solicit the honour of your permission to declare the eternal devotion which he vows to your accomplished Daughter, Miss Elizabeth. His expectations from his Uncle, and other contingencies, he entreats an early enterview to set before you. I enter, therefore, into none of those particulars; but cannot conclude without begging to add my sincere testimony to the many virtues which modesty else might conceal in this truly exemplary young man. "I have the honour to be, Sir.

"your most obedient Servent

"John Dervis."

MR WATTS: Why you see, now, he says nothing of his being a Lord. He only puts plain John.

ELIZA: How extraordinary! why has he not written himself? *(Aside.)*

55

MR WATTS: Are you sure, sir, as to that article of his being a Lord?

VALET: 'Pon my honour, sir.

MRS WATTS: Well, I declare I wonder you can ask sich a question, Tommy. Why one may see it's from a Lord as plain as can be.

MISS WATTS: Yes, it's exact the Lord. I should know it for a Lord's anywhere.

MR WATTS: Well, sir, you'll be kind enough to take it back to his Lordship Lord John Dervis and tell Lord John Dervis his Lordship that my darter says –

ELIZA: No – Stop! – hold – my dear Father –

MR WATTS: Why what is all this, Betsey? Have you changed your mind?

ELIZA: I will explain myself fully, if you will only have the goodness to defer any answer till you have heard me – one moment – alone.

MR WATTS: Why then, my dear, let's ask the gentleman to take a turn or two the t'other way.

VALET: O Pray, sir, – ladies – no apology. *(Walks to some distance.)*

MISS WATTS: He's just as pelite as a Lord Himself. I dare say he's the particular friend of Lord John Dervis.

MRS WATTS: Well, but, Elizenanny, my dear, I suppose your Mamma may stay to hear you?

ELIZA: You are very right, my dear Mother –

MISS WATTS: And I'm sure I shan't go, for I want to know what it is myself.

ELIZA: This letter I now fancy – I now begin to believe – I now –

MISS WATTS: La, Sister Eliziana, what makes you stutter so?

ELIZA: This letter, I now fancy, has been written…I rather imagine…at the request of – of – of a gentleman that –

MISS WATTS: Of a gentleman? La, who?

ELIZA: About a year ago, a Mr Cleveland came over to Calcutta…in a very advantageous post – and happened to form a particular intimacy with Mr Alderson – and in short my dear Father…

MISS WATTS: La, if I don't believe you was going to be married to him?

MRS WATTS: Well, that's pretty enough.

MR WATTS: But what has he got, my dear?

ELIZA: Indulge him, sir, with an interview. He entertains the most reasonable expectations of inheritance from his uncle Sir Marmaduke Tylney.

MR WATTS: Expectations, my dear, did not make me one farthing of my fortune. However, if he had old Alderson of his side, most likely he has something of substance, so I shan't object to the seeing of him.

MISS WATTS: Ask him to dinner, then, Pa'; and ask the lord to come with him. And ask that smart gentleman.

MRS WATTS: No, no, tea will do very well, my dear. No need to be giving away one's dinners at sich a rate as that.

MISS WATTS: La, Ma', you're always so stingy!

MR WATTS: No, no, I shall ask him to call some morning. That's quite enough till I know what he's got. Sir! Sir! I say –

VALET: *(Returning.)* At your commands, sir.

MR WATTS: If you should happen to see Lord John Dervis his Lordship agen, sir –

VALET: O yes, sir! I always see my Lord when he dresses.

MR WATTS: Dresses?

VALET: He'd make but a poor hand without me, I believe!

MISS WATTS: La!

MRS WATTS: Dear! – Why sure, sir, you a'nt the footman?

VALET: Footman? O no ma'am! I am my Lord's valet.

MRS WATTS: Dear, Peggy, how could you be took in so?

MISS WATTS: La, Ma', it was all you! I thought he looked something quite mean at the first. And I was just going to say so, only something put it out of my head. I'll assure him! to sit himself down on the same bench with us!

MR WATTS: Well, well, my dear, time was I was not half as good. Mr Walley, you'll tell his Lordship Lord John Dervis I can't write, because of being in Kinsington Gardens; but my Darter does not deny to knowing of Muster Cleveland, and so, that being the case, he may call when it happens to suit.

VALET: Sir, your very obedient! Ladies, – yours.

Exit bowing.

MR WATTS: He's a deal genteeler than I! I can't make that kereless bow for my life. I'm always afeard of a tumble. Why, if my eyes don't deceive me, if there i'nt Cousin Joel Tibbs! why Cousin Joel! Joel Tibbs!

Exit.

MISS WATTS: La, Pa'! What do you call him for? Come, Sister Eliziana, let's sit down here. If he should speak to us before anybody, let's pretend not to know him.

ELIZA: O Cleveland! that once I were but yours!

MISS WATTS: Well, now let's talk. Pray how long may you have had this lover?

ELIZA: Pardon me, Sister; the narrative just now would extremely oppress me. Will you take this seat, madam?

MRS WATTS: Thankee, my dear, I don't care if I do; for my new shoes are so strait over my toes –

MISS WATTS: Why now what do you offer it for? Now we can't talk without her hearing us!

ELIZA: I would rather not sit. Heavens! Cleveland! With a lady! Arm in arm! It must be his Sister. O that he were alone! that I could learn his plans. I will keep in sight, yet leave it to his own discretion to address me or not.

Enter CLEVELAND and JEMIMA.

JEMIMA: I comprehend you perfectly, my dear Brother; but pray detain me no longer. Miss Percival is waiting for me. I give you my word, to be your messenger to Bond Street the first moment I can command the chariot.

CLEVELAND: Go in a chair, my dear Jemima. Do any thing rather than lose time. Send her in these lines: I am sure she will not refuse their request to grant me a short audience without delay.

JEMIMA: But what will Lady Wilhelmina say to my bringing a total stranger –

CLEVELAND: Jemima! 'Tis Eliza – standing by that seat – O look! Is she not most lovely?

JEMIMA: Her appearance is extremely interesting.

CLEVELAND: How fortunate an incident! I can now present you to each other, and tell her all my difficulties at once.

JEMIMA: But stop! – Who are those people with her? They look immensely odd.

MISS PERCIVAL rushes in, and, catching the hand of JEMIMA throws herself against the shoulder of CLEVELAND, without looking at him.

MISS PERCIVAL: O Jemima! – I am in a terror – an alarm – an agitation – I have been so dreadfully affrighted –

JEMIMA: But how, my dear Miss Percival?

MISS PERCIVAL: I flew from the carriage to – your arms! – Bless me! Is it not you that are supporting me? Who have I been leaning against? I am all tremor and confusion.

JEMIMA: Let us go back together to the chariot.

MISS PERCIVAL: *(Looking up.)* O all ye stars! What have I done? Traiterous Jemima! you have betrayed me into the arms of – your Brother! – I fly! I fly!

She runs away.

CLEVELAND: How perverse an encounter!

MISS PERCIVAL: *(Stopping.)* O succour – succour me!

CLEVELAND: From what madam?

MISS PERCIVAL: O I can't speak! I have seen such a frightful sight – Support me to a seat. My feet totter.

She swoons. CLEVELAND and JEMIMA lead her to the nearest seat.

JEMIMA: Dear Miss Percival, what has terrified you?

MISS PERCIVAL: O, two monsters! two shocking monsters, in something resembling human shape that, had I not fled hither for refuge, I really think they must have demolished me with horror.

CLEVELAND: Amazing!

MISS PERCIVAL: Now do both of you sit down by me till I am a little recovered.

JEMIMA sits; CLEVELAND only bows.

And now, do pray, Jemima, ask your Brother to tell me one thing sincerely. Does not he think me a terrible coward?

JEMIMA: What say you Brother?

CLEVELAND: Not absolutely an amazon, undoubtedly, madam.

MISS PERCIVAL: Pho! – Ask him, Jemima, if he does not think it very silly to be so fearful?

JEMIMA: Well, Brother?

CLEVELAND: I never judge a lady by any single trait.

MISS PERCIVAL: I protest if I hear one more such priggish answer, I shall yawn till tomorrow! Ask him – no, this one thing I must ask myself, for 'tis of the utmost moment. Pray, Mr Cleveland tell me, solemnly, have you, or have you not a serious aversion to wigs?

CLEVELAND: To wigs?

JEMIMA: To wigs?

MISS PERCIVAL: Yes, for old men, I mean – if you would not rather encounter a brigand – a felon, – an assassin; I can never speak to you more. Why don't you answer? What in nature can you be contemplating?

Turning round she perceives MRS and MISS WATTS, who obscure her view of ELIZA.

Heavens, what creatures! How can you bear to look at them?

CLEVELAND: Me? – I – I – I scarcely saw them. *(Turning hastily away.)*

MISS PERCIVAL: Did you ever see such drolly horrid frights?

CLEVELAND: I really – have not taken – much notice of them.

MISS PERCIVAL: What can thus abash and confound him? *(Apart.)* O but do look. She certainly fancies we are admiring her. Now don't be so cruel as to turn your eyes another way.

CLEVELAND: *(Apart to JEMIMA.)* Dearest Jemima, persuade her to depart, I beseech you!

JEMIMA: *(Apart to CLEVELAND.)* Propose handing her to the chariot.

CLEVELAND: How tormenting! *(Apart.)* May I not be allowed – Madam – to have the honour – to – to conduct you to your carriage?

MISS PERCIVAL: If he were not so embarrassed, I should think him an Iseecle. I must try to give him a little courage. *(Aside.)* Well, I'll endeavour to rise. Your arm, Jemima. Heavens, how weak your arm is! Cleveland! will you not help to sustain me?

She rises between CLEVELAND and JEMIMA, and is moving from the seat; but starts suddenly back.

O heavens! O all ye stars! The monsters! The monsters!

JEMIMA: Where? – What? – Where? –

CLEVELAND: I see nothing.

MISS PERCIVAL: The Wigs! The very Wigs!

Enter MR WATTS and MR TIBBS.

MISS PERCIVAL: Do you not see them? Look! look there! they approach! – ah! some drops.

She swoons in the arms of CLEVELAND.

CLEVELAND: I see nothing in the World.

MR WATTS: Now which way can they be gadded to?

MR TIBBS: Why, there! look yonder, man! Cousin Aylce! Cousin Peg! And you, too my little Betsey! Dears, I'm afeard there's a lady taken bad. Pray, ma'am –

MISS PERCIVAL: O frightful! one of the Wigs is fixing me!

MR TIBBS: Belike the lady's subject to fits?

MRS WATTS: *(Advancing.)* Well, if she is, do you get to t'other side, for I know a way to cure her in a minnet. It's only just the littlest touch in the World of the top of the nose, with the tip of the finger; and if the young lady –

MISS WATTS: *(Following.)* La, Ma', can't you let me –

MISS PERCIVAL: O the Savages are bearing down upon us!

Runs off, one hand covering her face, the other holding CLEVELAND's hand.

CLEVELAND: How torturing an incident!

Exit.

JEMIMA: What an extraordinary set! Can Frank's new Relations be worse?

Exit.

MISS WATTS: La, Ma', what did you talk of touching her nose for? Now you've frightened her off. Do, Sister Eliziana, come along with me, and let's see which way she turns.

Exit.

MRS WATTS: Why, now, I'm sure, my dear, – Why how you go on without hearing one! I'm sure I wish I had not bought these new shoes.

Exit, hobbling. Leaving MR WATTS, MR TIBBS and ELIZA, who keeps walking aloof.

MR TIBBS: Why now I should be glad to know what that young lady gave that squall for, upon my coming up to her; just as if I'd been something out of the way!

MR WATTS: My dear Cousin Tibbs, the great World is full of them things. You can't make 'em out no how. I could tell you such stories of how rude people's been to me, as would make you think nothing of anything.

MR TIBBS: Why then, why a'n't you as rude to them?

MR WATTS: O, it's surprising what they'll do. Why how do you think I was served one day by a gentleman of Darter's acquaintance – but come a little this way, for fear of Betsey; for if she should tell Peg what I'm saying, she'll La, Pa', me for half an hour. It's a very troublesome thing the having darters.

Exeunt. ELIZA alone.

ELIZA: How strange an adventure! They could not both be his sisters – yet how familiar a conduct to anyone but a Brother! I could hear nothing; but all I saw was most extraordinary. O Cleveland! with elegance like yours, founded on birth, education and intellectual endowments, can I wonder if your mind should involuntarily recoil from an alliance, in which shame must continually struggle against kindness, and Pride against Happiness?

Enter MR WATTS and MR TIBBS.

MR WATTS: Betsey, my dear, our coach is up ready, and your sister says we must go, for there's no company, she says, this morning. So we're all going. Only do you walk on first, my dear. There, that way, – don't you see 'em?

Exit ELIZA.

MR WATTS: Take my advice, Cousin Tibbs, and never be over persuaded by your wife and darters to leave off business.

MR TIBBS: Why, what a dickens, Tom, a'n't you happy, then, with your fine coach to rock you to sleep from one end of

London to t'other? And your fine house that makes you look like a lodger in it? And your fine servants standing by one by two, by three, to stare an old friend out of countenance? And your fine cloaths, that nobody can know you in?

MR WATTS: Ah, Joel, as long as business did but go on, all them things was a joy to me! For then I was somebody! And my wife and darter did not dare give themselves such airs. I used to speak as sharp as they. But now it's nothing but La, Pa'! at every word. I can never talk two minutes together, but what I'm sure to say something wrong. They've made me give up all my old acquaintance, because of their being so mean; and as to our new ones, it's as plain as ever you see they only despise me: for they never take off their hats if I meet them in the streets; and they never get up off their chairs, if I ask them how they do in their own houses; and they never give me a word of answer I can make out, if I put a question to them.

MR TIBBS: Why then don't take off your hat to them; and don't get off your chair to them; and don't answer them when they speak to you. That's the way I should treat 'em, if any of 'em came across me. I should like nothing better.

MR WATTS: O, but you've no notion what it is, living in the great World! There's nothing going on but spending. One can't wear a coat for a couple of years, but what it's quite out of the mode! They'll turn you off a hat, before you can well know if it's been on your head! And if you talk to any of 'em of getting a shoe mended, or anything a little saving, they'll stare at you as if you was out of your mind.

MR TIBBS: They might stare like stuck pigs for aught I should care. Why, I declare –

MR WATTS: But I must not make my wife wait. If you can come to me tonight, Cousin Joel, I'll sure be in my little parlour while my wife's upstairs. Only remember this, Cousin Joel – never leave off business!

Exit. MR TIBBS alone.

MR TIBBS: Poor Tom! So he's only got all this money to be put out of his place, and held up as one may say, for a laughing stock to be made fun of! Why I, now, that am but a poor man by his side, though time was I could have counted a guinea to his sixpence, I'd no more be trampled upon, at that rate, and elbowed, and flouted, and grinned at, as he says he catches 'em doing, than I'd be made the Pope of Rome. Why what's a Lord, and a Baronight, and Squire, and that to me? Not but what if they'll be pelite, I'll be pelite too, but, fegs, if they ben't – well! We'll see! We'll see!

ACT IV

Later, that same afternoon.

JEMIMA's dressing room at Sir Marmaduke Tylney's. Enter JEMIMA, leading in ELIZA.

JEMIMA: I left him seeking you, with the utmost anxiety, in Kensington Gardens. He will be here, I am certain, almost immediately. I will not, therefore, anticipate his communications; he wishes, I know, to relate his difficulties to you himself.

ELIZA: Alas, I can too easily imagine what they may be!

JEMIMA: Be assured –

LADY WILHELMINA: *(Within.)* A young lady, do you say

JEMIMA: 'Tis Lady Wilhelmina!

ELIZA: Lady Wilhelmina?

Enter LADY WILHELMINA.

LADY WILHELMINA: Allow me, Miss Cleveland, to enquire – but I beg pardon – I interrupt you – I intrude? *(Looking at ELIZA.)*

ELIZA: *(Curtseying respectfully.)* It is I, rather, who intrude madam, and – and –

LADY WILHELMINA: Who have you got here Miss Cleveland? What is this young woman? *(Apart to JEMIMA, but always erectly staring at ELIZA.)*

ELIZA: Perhaps *(To JEMIMA.)* I had better have the honour of waiting upon you some other time?

LADY WILHELMINA: By no means. I beg I may not be in your way. Don't let me give you any uneasiness. Who is it, I say? *(To JEMIMA in a half whisper.)*

JEMIMA: Ma'am, it's a lady that – that – a young lady that I saw – that I met just now – in Kensington Gardens, – and –

LADY WILHELMINA: In Kensington Gardens?

JEMIMA: Yes, ma'am; Miss Percival took me to Kensington Gardens, and – and –

LADY WILHELMINA: If this young lady is an acquaintance of Miss Percival, how astonishingly awkward, Miss Cleveland, not to introduce me to her!

JEMIMA: Ma'am, I –

ELIZA: I beg –

LADY WILHELMINA: Can anybody under my roof be so uninformed how to conduct themselves? You really make me blush for you, Miss Cleveland. I hope, however, madam *(Advancing smilingly and bowing her head to ELIZA.)*, you will have the goodness to forgive her. She means perfectly well; nobody means better; but she is not yet entirely all I could wish. Give me leave, madam, to have the honour of hoping Miss Percival is well?

ELIZA: Miss Percival, madam?

JEMIMA: 'Tis a mistake that will delay all enquiry; let it pass a few minutes, I conjure you! *(Apart to ELIZA.)*

LADY WILHELMINA: Whispering too? You really make me nervous, Miss Cleveland! But you will allow, I hope, madam *(To ELIZA.)*, for early disadvantages. It is only within these very few years that I have been favoured with the company of Miss Cleveland under my own roof; for, till my alliance with Sir Marmaduke, we were nearly strangers to each other. This you might, indeed, have conjectured.

JEMIMA: I hope so! *(Aside.)*

LADY WILHELMINA: You, madam, whose elegant deportment immediately announces your own connexions to be in the very first style –

ELIZA: Mine, ma'am? –

LADY WILHELMINA: I never mistake in that particular.

Enter SIR MARMADUKE.

Permit me, Sir Marmaduke, to present to you a friend of Miss Percival's.

ELIZA: Indeed, ma'am, your La'ship – *(JEMIMA stops her.)*

SIR MARMADUKE: Miss Percival and her friends have us wholly at their command. Where's my Nephew?

LADY WILHELMINA: I imagine with Miss Percival. At least he has kept me waiting two hours and three quarters in my dressing room; and I can devise no other excuse for such inattention.

SIR MARMADUKE: Happy young rascal! Ah, I told him what it was to be a happy young rascal!

ELIZA: With Miss Percival?

LADY WILHELMINA: Unless, indeed, he is yet more nobly employed for us all, in trying to invalidate his brother's disgraceful purpose of bringing that City-born girl into our family.

SIR MARMADUKE: If she pays his debts, what's where she's born to us?

LADY WILHELMINA: How any young person of that class can even think of coming among Us, often amazes me. What is it possible persons of that description can expect from Us?

ELIZA: Miss Cleveland – suffer me, I beg, to retire.

JEMIMA: No, no! *(Holding her.)*

SIR MARMADUKE: Everybody knows those kind of matches are mere things of convenience, Lady Wil: and as to Frank – who ever expected to hear anything better from such a prodigal? If Cleveland indeed had taken up with a girl of low extraction 'twould have nettled me; but Cleveland, ah! happy young rascal! – Give me leave, ma'am *(To ELIZA.)*, to commend myself to Miss Percival through your favour; and to assure her I have not forgotten her kind invitation to Piccadilly this evening.

ELIZA: Sir – I – *(JEMIMA stops her.)*

SIR MARMADUKE: And now I must get ready.

Exit.

LADY WILHELMINA: It is impossible we should any of us forget what it is so much our happiness to remember as an invitation to Miss Percival's. And permit me, madam, to hope I may there have the honour of confirming an acquaintance which I saw, in its very opening, would prove of the first class. I never mistake in that point.

Exit.

ELIZA: Ah, madam! I see plainly that his situation, with respect to me, is unacknowledged to any part of his family but yourself! O Cleveland! so soon have you learnt to blush for her who so lately you delighted to exalt and to honour? Pardon me, madam – my heart is full.

JEMIMA: Let me, then, instantly explain –

ELIZA: I would fain begone; but my Father promised to call for me –

Enter MISS PERCIVAL.

MISS PERCIVAL: O Jemima, I die! do you know that Wretch – O you are not alone? – Pardon me.

ELIZA: Is there any other room where –

JEMIMA: By no means. This is a young lady, Miss Percival – that – that –

MISS PERCIVAL: O, I beg her pardon a thousand times. I hope she'll excuse my wild manner. That Wretch, my dear Jemima, desires a private audience. How abominable! As if I could ever bear to see him alone!

ELIZA: I am sure I must incommode you. Pray, Miss Cleveland –

MISS PERCIVAL: O no, not in the least, I assure you. Nobody minds what I say. I rattle in all sort of ways. But Jemima, is it not very presuming? What shall I do to punish him? See! he has had the impertinence to write to me. Tell me if ever you saw so priggish a little note in your life. See me alone? What can he mean? Can you form any guess, Jemima?

JEMIMA: I think – I can!

MISS PERCIVAL: O tell me, then! – no don't – I won't know. Only don't fail to inform him I shan't write an answer. And as to seeing him and alone – I feel fainting at the very idea! Give me back the Wretch's note. Well, what makes you so insipid, Jemima? Why don't you tell me what to do? Are you in the Creature's confidence?

JEMIMA: Sometimes – But I knew not this part of his plan.

MISS PERCIVAL: What part do you know, then? Pray tell me quick. I can't live a moment in any suspense. What part of his plan do you know? Do you think he dares ever imagine anything about me? O frightful! If you say yes, I shall certainly shut myself up! – But where? There are no Convents, now. Where can one be shut up, Jemima? What a barbarous thing it is Jemima, that one has no shelter from those odious monsters the Men! I wish one could find some uninhabited Island, to which one could retreat from them in a Mass. But perhaps they would only pursue one. Men are amazing plagues. Do you think, Jemima, your Brother would take that trouble?

ELIZA: Heavens! Cleveland! *(Aside.)*

MISS PERCIVAL: Do you know I begin to take a great aversion to men. I am really afraid I shall quite hate them soon. And that will be very inconvenient, for one can't avoid sometimes seeing them. Do you hate them Jemima?

JEMIMA: Not – All!

MISS PERCIVAL: Why I'm not sure if I hate them All myself. But what in the World do you think this horrid creature will say to me, if I should trust him with an interview? Can you fancy to yourself what would be his subject? I am afraid this young lady thinks me very odd.

ELIZA: I know not what to conjecture. *(Aside.)*

Enter MR WATTS.

MISS PERCIVAL: Ah! – one of my Wigs! Hide me dear Jemima – and be sure let it be where your Brother cannot find me!

Exit running.

JEMIMA: Excuse me, a moment, dear madam. *(To ELIZA.)* I am glad to get her away!

Aside and exit.

MR WATTS: Why Betsey, my dear! why I hope I don't make the young lady run away? I only come upstairs to tell you – the young gentleman as got the lord to write me the letter, is below.

ELIZA: The young gentleman, sir?

MR WATTS: Why, as soon as I got home from setting you down, who should I see in the Entry a waiting, but he? So when he told me he was the young Muster Cleveland as came to court you, I told him I had just set you down at his Sister's here; so nothing would content him, but our both coming after you together.

Exit.

ELIZA: O Cleveland! how critical is this moment! – and how happy should it clear away the dreadful suspicions that nearly overpower me!

Enter FRANK CLEVELAND together with MR WATTS.

ELIZA: Good Heaven! who is this?

MR WATTS: Now, sir, here's my Darter; and now I'm ready to hear what you've got to offer.

FRANK: *(In poetic vein.)* Enchanting Fair! what exquisite happiness is mine to pay you thus my homage under this next-to-paternal roof!

ELIZA: What can this mean?

FRANK: Surely all the Elements – O Elements kind and fair! – united to forward my hopes, when they wafted to our sea-girt coast the destined object of my wishes! And surely …surely…what the Devil shall I say next? *(Aside.)*

ELIZA: Sir!

FRANK: Surely, I say madam, surely – surely if Love be the divine gift of felicity, the fates ordained my bliss upon the very hour you first set sail from India's soil.

MR WATTS: I dare say he i'n't worth a groat, he's got such a fluent tongue. *(Aside.)*

FRANK: Indeed, if it be possible to imagine bliss more – more – more joyful than mine – it must be – it must be – it must certainly be, I say – very – very extraordinary, indeed. – Rather lame that! *(Aside.)*

MR WATTS: I've no opinion of him. *(Aside.)*

ELIZA: Pray, my dear Father!!

FRANK: But if the most fervent devotion – the most tender homage – the most timid adoration, can move a fair bosom to gentle sympathy, then shall I not find my ardent hopes all blasted, and blighted, and nipt in the opening bud. – Very well that, indeed! *(Aside.)*

MR WATTS: I dare to say he's a Swindler.

Takes a news-paper and sits in a corner reading.

ELIZA: How incomprehensible is this! Allow me, sir, to enquire why you address me in so singular a style?

FRANK: Ma'am?

ELIZA: If it is merely for sport –

FRANK: Sport, madam? – Ye Gods! – I had flattered myself, by your obliging attention to my blushing overtures, that I had your own fair permission for paying you my obsequious devoirs.

ELIZA: Overtures, sir? Good Heaven! – was that note to my Father from you?

FRANK: From my friend, ma'am, my Lord John Dervis.

ELIZA: And meant for you? – Amazing! – I thought – I imagined – it had been written for – for – Mr Cleveland?

FRANK: It was so, my dear madam.

ELIZA: How strange! Is your name, then Cleveland, sir?

FRANK: Most humbly at your command, madam.

ELIZA: Probably then, – permit me, sir, to ask – if you have – a brother?

FRANK: I have, ma'am: just returned, like your fair self, from the East Indies.

ELIZA: The East Indies?

FRANK: Yes, ma'am; and who is now upon that very pinnacle to which my fairest ambition rises; the pinnacle, madam, of connubial happiness.

ELIZA: How wonderful! Can he behave thus yet know his Brother's situation? *(Aside.)* Will you allow me, sir, to make one more enquiry?

FRANK: How she softens! She's a good pretty Girl, really. *(Aside.)* Allow, madam? Ordain, enjoin, command, insist.

ELIZA: Has your Brother the slightest idea of the sort of discourse you now hold to me?

FRANK: Idea? He was the first confidant of my budding wishes, and your full-blown victory. I don't know how I shall get on much longer! *(Aside.)*

ELIZA: O Cleveland! have you but urged me hither to make me over to your brother *(Aside.)*

FRANK: I have it now. *(Aside.)* Well may the East be celebrated for its fragrance, if thence issue Flowers of such exquisite odour! well may it supply Incense to the World, if for Incense it offers such objects! well –

CLEVELAND: *(Within.)* Jemima! Jemima!

ELIZA: 'Tis Cleveland! How shall I bear to look at him? *(aside.)*

FRANK: What a plaguy interruption! I may never attain the same energy again! *(Aside.)*

Enter CLEVELAND.

CLEVELAND: *(In entering.)* Jemima, I have been barbarously detained – May I venture – *(To ELIZA who walks away and seats herself in a recess at the end of the scene.)*

73

FRANK: *(Following and stopping him.)* Prithee, Brother, go downstairs again!

CLEVELAND: Frank! In the name of Heaven, what is it you do here?

FRANK: Hush! Hush! don't you see? *(Pointing to ELIZA.)* Now do go down quick, there's a good fellow.

CLEVELAND: And on what pretence, sir, are you in this room with – with – with – without Jemima?

FRANK: I'll tell you some other opportunity; but just now, do pray make haste and leave us.

CLEVELAND: Us, sir? Whom do you presume to include by Us? What have you to do with – with – with such a word as Us?

FRANK: How troublesome you are! I'll explain it, all by and by, I tell you; mean time, do pray run downstairs. I want to be alone.

CLEVELAND: So do I, sir!

FRANK: That is, not actually alone – you – you understand me? *(Pointing to ELIZA.)*

CLEVELAND: If I do, may I die this instant!

FRANK: Why, then the climate of India has dullified all your senses! Can't you conceive, when you find a man engaged with a fair lady, that you may do twenty things more agreeable to either of them than to come and look on?

CLEVELAND: Engaged with a fair lady? – Do you pretend to be here, then, by any permission? Any authority but your own?

FRANK: To be sure I do! Did I not tell you how the affair stood? You have no memory, man!

CLEVELAND: This absurdity nearly maddens me! Prithee call Jemima.

FRANK: Call Jemima? Ha! Ha! facetious enough! And what for? To make a quartetto when a trio is already so out of season? Come, come, Brother, none of your jokes.

CLEVELAND: There is no enduring this trifling. What I cannot learn from you, I must solicit from this lady. Will you permit me – *(Advancing to ELIZA.)*

FRANK: *(Stopping him.)* Hold, hold man! what are you thinking of? You may do mischief irretrievable. Can't you guess who that is?

CLEVELAND: That?

FRANK: Why it's my little Cit.

CLEVELAND: What!

FRANK: My little Gentoo, that I told you of! Have you forgotten it all? My Betsey Watts.

CLEVELAND: Frank, you'll provoke me to –

FRANK: Nay, don't be in a passion before her face. The poor thing can't help being born a Cockney, or bred a Hottentot. And, really, if you could but look at her divested of your prejudice, you'd think her a good pretty girl yourself.

CLEVELAND: Frank, I swear – *(Raising his voice.)*

MR WATTS: *(Looking round.)* Anan!

FRANK: Hush, hush! what the Deuce do you speak so loud for? Now you've disturbed my Papa!

CLEVELAND: Who? *(Looking about.)*

FRANK: Nay, don't start and jump so. I tell you that's my Papa. He sits in that corner not to interrupt my soft speeches; for he has promised, if my Uncle will come down handsomely, not to oppose his Daughter's wishes.

CLEVELAND: His daughter's wishes?

FRANK: Yes. She was smit with me at a glance. The girl's not amiss in her taste. The old codger confessed himself she had owned her passion for me at the receipt of my proposals.

CLEVELAND: *(Stamping.)* Tis false!

MR WATTS: Anan, there? Hay? What? *(Coming forward.)*

FRANK: Now see what you've done! – Nothing, sir, but a little raillery of my Brother. He affects to doubt your kind concurrence in –

CLEVELAND: Doubt? No sir! pardon me, I cannot doubt, I feel certain of the impossibility of your listening, even for a minute, to proposals for your inestimable Daughter from an utter stranger.

MR WATTS: Stranger? Bless you, no! why this here young gentleman knew my darter in Indy.

CLEVELAND: What Frank?

FRANK: Brava, my little Cit! the Girl must have invented this to favour her sudden passion. *(Aside.)*

MR WATTS: Yes; he was old Mr Alderson's intimatest friend.

CLEVELAND: Really Frank? And do you assert Frank, you were acquainted with Mr Alderson?

FRANK: Hand and glove together!

CLEVELAND: And in India, sir? Was it in India you formed this friendship?

FRANK: In every part of the Globe alike. Whenever we met, we were equally cordial.

MR WATTS: Why I told you as much!

CLEVELAND: What gross imposition –

MR WATTS: Imposition? Why, Betsey, my dear, pray come this way. Did not you say that this here young gentleman was your sweetheart in Indy?

ELIZA: *(Advancing.)* No, sir, I know him not. I was under a very great mistake. I beseech that we may instantly go home where I will try to rectify it.

CLEVELAND: Poor Frank.

MR WATTS: Good lauk, not know him! Why, pray, sir, i'n't your name Cleveland?

FRANK: I have that small honour, sir.

MR WATTS: Why, my dear, didn't you say as Muster Cleveland –

ELIZA: I spoke in errour. I know him not, sir, believe me.

FRANK: Who, o – o – o – o!

CLEVELAND: Permit me, then, now to speak for myself; and suffer me, sir *(To MR WATTS.)* to entreat your sanction that I may address a few words in your hearing, to Miss Elizabeth.

MR WATTS: Servant, sir, servant! may I make bold first to ask your name, if it is not anywise disagreeable?

CLEVELAND: Cleveland, sir.

MR WATTS: Why, my dear, why now here's another of these Muster Cleveland's wants to speak to you. Pray do you hap to know him any better?

ELIZA: Once I thought I did! – but I find I judged too hastily. Indeed I know him not!

FRANK: Poor Cleveland!

CLEVELAND: Astonishing!

MR WATTS: Why there, now! Why my darter says she don't know neither one of you nor t'other!

FRANK: I wonder what the little Devil means! *(aside.)*

CLEVELAND: How can I thus deeply have offended her. *(Aside.)* Allow me, madam, at least –

Enter MISS PERCIVAL.

MISS PERCIVAL: Miss Cleveland! – bless me! I thought to have found Miss Cleveland – and I see nothing but men!

Enter JEMIMA.

JEMIMA: On the contrary, my dear Miss Percival, you know I told you –

MISS PERCIVAL: Hush! Hush! you abominable little mischief-maker!

ELIZA: Heavens! *(Aside.)* My dear Father, are you not ready?

MR WATTS: Yes, my dear, yes; I'll only just pop my eyes over this here one more advertisement. *(Reading.)*

MISS PERCIVAL: You don't tell me who that young lady is, Jemima. *(Apart to JEMIMA.)*

JEMIMA: A – a new friend.

MISS PERCIVAL: Of your own?

JEMIMA: I – I hope she will become so.

MISS PERCIVAL: I rather suspect – pray, Mr Frank, come hither. Let me speak to you in private. Do you think that young lady remarkably ugly?

FRANK: She stands so near to you, that I cannot judge.

JEMIMA: *(Apart to CLEVELAND.)* My dear Brother, do you not perceive the necessity of explaining with Miss Percival immediately! Do you not see the cruel mistake she is nourishing?

CLEVELAND: Alas! Jemima, the averted eyes of Eliza unfit me for everything! but I believe you are right, and if she will allow me an audience less public –

MISS PERCIVAL: Now what are you two plotting together? something about me, I dare say.

CLEVELAND: If, madam, I might presume to solicit a two minute's hearing –

ELIZA: My heart sinks! *(Aside.)* Have you not finished sir? *(To MR WATTS, who shakes his elbow in a token of a negative.)*

MISS PERCIVAL: Two minutes? Horrible! I expire at the very thought. Jemima, do tell the creature I can't possibly grant such a request. No! I cannot give him more than – one minute at the most! *(smiling at him.)*

ELIZA: Pardon me, Miss Cleveland, – I am pressed for time. I will wait for you sir, in the carriage. *(To MR WATTS.)*

Exit.

CLEVELAND: May I not conduct you to the coach?

FRANK: No, no; *(Holding him.)* Don't you see, she goes first, purposely to give me opportunity to speak to her without square toes? And to explain her caprice? Don't be in the way so, man! look to your own affairs!

Exit.

MISS PERCIVAL: *(Patting him on the sleeve as he is following.)* I am sure Frank has some design that way. Don't be a Marplot, Cleveland!

CLEVELAND: I shall lose my senses! *(Aside.)*

MR WATTS: *(Looking around.)* Why what's this, now? Is my Darter gone? Why then I've no business to stay behind, I'm sure. Ladies and gentlemen, your humble servant, sir. And yours, ma'am. And your's too, ma'am.

Exit, bowing awkwardly around.

MISS PERCIVAL: Bless me, Jemima, what's that man? Did you ever in your life see such an animal? And who is the fair Nymph? some curiosity found out by Frank, I make no doubt.

CLEVELAND: How shall I contain my rage? *(Aside.)*

MISS PERCIVAL: Your Brother's grown horribly stupid, Jemima.

JEMIMA: *(Apart to CLEVELAND.)* Seize this moment for an explanation with Miss Percival, Brother.

Exit.

MISS PERCIVAL waits expectantly. Re-enter FRANK CLEVELAND.

MISS PERCIVAL: I'm glad you're returned, Frank, to keep us awake. Do pray tell me who that Quiz is!

FRANK: Don't ask me, I beg you.

MISS PERCIVAL: Not ask you? – Why?

FRANK: Because I'm confoundedly out of countenance about him.

MISS PERCIVAL: Out of countenance about him, are you? Ah, ha! then I have conjectured right. And where, in Fortune's name, did you light upon these two Things?

FRANK: Why I'll tell you the story, for it's really a good one.

CLEVELAND: May I entreat –

MISS PERCIVAL: No, no; I must hear the story first. Well, Frank?

CLEVELAND: Is it utterly impossible, madam, to hope for the honour of a single moment's hearing?

MISS PERCIVAL: Heavens Cleveland, don't speak in that solemn tone! Do tell on, Frank.

FRANK: Why, really, the adventure's amusing enough. Only my Brother has taken an unaccountable antipathy to it. This little Thing, you must know, is just returned from the East Indies –

MISS PERCIVAL: From the East Indies, and not married? That's a bad sign! There must be some terrible flaw. Have a care, Frank!

CLEVELAND: I shall run wild! *(Aside.)*

FRANK: The sign may be bad, I grant, but the effect is tolerable enough: she has brought over eighty thousand pounds at her sole disposal.

MISS PERCIVAL: And you, I presume, have the kindness to propose taking the trouble and management of this sum out of her hands?

FRANK: Why a lady may employ herself so much better than as a Steward, that I have not been without a little thought that way. However, I am not fixed. My Brother is so inordinately offended by the vulgarity of the connexion –

CLEVELAND: I offended at the vulgarity – at the – I? –

FRANK: He is ready to annihilate me every time I name it. I've only to hint at my little Lizzy Watts –

CLEVELAND: Desist, if you please, sir, once and for all from naming her anymore!

MISS PERCIVAL: Bless me, how passionate!

FRANK: O, he has set his heart so completely against the poor little Girl, that I foresee, if I persevere, an inevitable breach, unless your charitable influence –

MISS PERCIVAL: My influence! my Command. Fie upon it Cleveland! how can you be so squeamish? For my part, I doat upon a little excentricity. Why should we be All born alike? Besides, think how amusing to see her and the Quiz contrasted with Lady Wil! If you don't place me where I may witness the first interview, Frank, I'll never forgive you. Won't it be delicious, Cleveland? Why, bless me, why should you let it affect you so?

CLEVELAND: Intolerable! – My head turns round! madam –

MISS PERCIVAL: Nay, nay, what signifies Frank's wife? Not but what Frank is a very good Frank, but still, why may he not please himself? – why may he not be indulged? If she is vulgar, Frank is good natured. He'll let you laugh, I'm sure – and let me laugh too; for I think nothing half so comical. If she is pettish, also, I shall never want Sel Volatile again; and if she is pert –

CLEVELAND: She – she is an Angel!

MISS PERCIVAL: What? Hay? did your Brother speak, Frank?

FRANK: Upon my honour, my Brother has been so extraordinary, that I won't take upon me to say whether he spoke or not; for why, all of a sudden, he should dub her an angel, – after so haughtily despising her –

CLEVELAND: Despising her? I despise? – no I adore her.

MISS PERCIVAL: How?

FRANK: Give me leave, in my turn, sir, to ask, now, whom it is you speak of?

CLEVELAND: Of one whom I regard as my Wife! – one whom I love to distraction! – one –

MISS PERCIVAL: Oh! *(Screams.)*

CLEVELAND: Pardon! Pardon! – I know not what I say.

FRANK: No more you have, all this morning. I'll bear witness for you to that.

CLEVELAND: I am in the deepest confusion – but I have been tortured out of all propriety. I dare not, madam, now address you; I am choked by my own abruptness. But my feelings have been worked so cruelly, that every barrier of prudence and every consideration of delicacy, are irresistibly broken down by invincible, imperious Truth. Pardon – pardon me!

CLEVELAND exits.

MISS PERCIVAL: Frank!

FRANK: Miss Percival!

MISS PERCIVAL: What can he mean?

FRANK: Nay, I don't know; but I begin to have a plaguy suspicion I can guess.

MISS PERCIVAL: An Angel? Love her to distraction – If I could believe him in earnest –

FRANK: Twenty things now recur, to make me wonder at my own supineness in not conjecturing there was some connexion immediately.

MISS PERCIVAL: Connexion?

FRANK: They both arrive from the East Indies, and at the same time – but what a Devil of a thing to be thus choused out of eighty thousand pounds, at the very moment –

MISS PERCIVAL: You treat this affair with tolerable levity, Mr Frank; but give me leave to tell you should an insult of this nature be really intended for me, you in common with the rest of your family, may learn to consider it more seriously. *(Going.)*

FRANK: Don't be offended with us All, dear madam. Distinguish the innocent from the guilty. Who, in this discovery and disappointment is so great a sufferer as myself?

MISS PERCIVAL: A sufferer? upon my word! Do you suppose me, then, a Sufferer? Give me leave to ask what it is you may imagine to be my loss?

FRANK: How charming a spirit! The very type and counterpart of my own! Our situations, and our humours –

MISS PERCIVAL: Sir!

FRANK: Nay there's no denying the agreeable sympathy of our positions.

MISS PERCIVAL: What impertinence! – But if you, sir – or any part of your family – imagine that the whole of your race is not detestable to me – you – they – and all of you will soon learn of your errour – For though I feel nothing in this business but insensibility – indifference – apathy – I yet know what is due to myself – and never will rest till I am vindicated.

FRANK: My own exact sensation upon the subject.

MISS PERCIVAL: This is no season, sir, for frivolous raillery. You will please to acquaint your Sister – no! tell her nothing – but inform your Brother – no I will not deign him any message. He shall feel, unanticipated, my resentment, and my hate! *(Going.)*

FRANK: Stop, dear madam! you give the exact process of what passes in my own mind. I find an absolute necessity of revenge. Not, indeed, of blood and slaughter; I won't meddle with bowls and daggers, – but I can never cast this business into the dulcest shades of oblivion, till I make them both feel at least as foolish as myself.

MISS PERCIVAL: Do you think you can do that?

FRANK: I'll do my best, and certainly not sleep till I succeed. The drowsy poppy would serve but to make me dance a jig, till I have turned upon themselves the tables of mockery and mortification.

MISS PERCIVAL: O Frank! Dear, delightful Frank, if you will but do that, and make Me the instrument of their humiliation and confusion, I shall adore you!

FRANK: Shall you faith! Why then so shall I you! which I have often longed to do before, but never dared. – Ah, my fair Miss Percival! how much sweeter a retaliation might we find for these offenders, than merely giving them back our torment!

MISS PERCIVAL: Pho, pho! now don't begin to be odious, the very first moment I find you endurable.

FRANK: Nay, as to that, my dear, madam, I assure you that I have so little natural propensity to connubial bliss – that I only dropt the hint to prove to you my personal respect.

MISS PERCIVAL: If you were less ridiculous, your insolence would be insupportable. But tell me this moment what we can do?

FRANK: I hesitate whether to sketch them for a Caricature, or to portray them in a Farce.

MISS PERCIVAL: You are the most divine creature under the Sun! Follow me instantly to Piccadilly. I shall be senseless before morning if I attempt to pass the night with such an indignity unrequited.

FRANK: I am proud to attend you; and pray don't forget that, should you, at last, prefer to confound the traitor by a supplanter – my scruple against the state shall not, in so particular a case, stand in the way.

MISS PERCIVAL: I could kill you for your effrontery, – if you were not, just now, so useful to me.

FRANK: 'Tis my standing maxim to sacrifice myself to my friends. *(Bowing.)*

MISS PERCIVAL: No nonsense! no nonsense!

Running off.

FRANK: Does she fly, now, to escape – or to be pursued? Modesty! thou art but a maidenly virtue – don't stand in the way of a young man's preferment! – I'll go ask her!

ACT V

That evening. An elegantly fitted-up apartment at MISS PERCIVAL'S, splendidly illuminated.

LORD JOHN: *(Within.)* If Frank Cleveland's here, I want to speak with him.

SERVANT: Please to walk upstairs, my Lord, and I'll see.

Enter LORD JOHN and SERVANT.

LORD JOHN: O the plague! What do you bring me hither for? I only want to speak with Frank Cleveland.

SERVANT: He was in this room just now, my Lord.

LORD JOHN: Ask if he's gone. But harkee! Don't say anything to Miss Percival of my being here. I would not disturb her. *(Exit SERVANT.)* The D–l a word could I find to say to her. I hate talking. *(Whistles.)*

Re-enter SERVANT.

SERVANT: Mr Cleveland has been gone some time, my Lord.

LORD JOHN: The Deuce he has? Well, if he should happen to call again before I catch him, tell him I want to speak to him consumedly. Something of moment. Where the D–l shall I go now?

Exit. Enter MISS PERCIVAL.

MISS PERCIVAL: Who's that?

SERVANT: Lord John Dervis, ma'am.

MISS PERCIVAL: What did you let him in for?

SERVANT: Ma'am, he –

MISS PERCIVAL: Don't answer! I can't bear to be answered. Go! – Stop! – If Frank Cleveland calls again, I'll see him. Nobody else. Yes, – stay! I expect the Tylney tribe. You must let them in. Nobody else. Go! – No, stop! If any queer-looking bodies come, you must not send 'em away. I don't know their names. Nobody else. Go, now –. Stay a minute! I have something I want to say. No; I've forgotten it. Go, can't you?

Exit SERVANT.

MISS PERCIVAL: What unspeakable pleasure it would give me to see that Wretch torn by wild beasts! And yet, were it not for the disgrace, the horrible disgrace, I should rejoice to have got rid of him, for he is grown so insipid, he made my head ache by his stupidity. But then – not to wait to be rejected! – A male creature, – destined for nothing but to die at one's feet. –

Enter FRANK.

MISS PERCIVAL: Well, Frank, what ages you have been gone! Where have you been slumbering all this time? What have you done? Will they come? Have you had any success? If not, run out of my house directly.

FRANK: Can you form a wish in vain? They will all wait upon you.

MISS PERCIVAL: You enchant me! Dear Frank, you are the very best Friend I have upon Earth. I hate everybody else breathing. How did you manage? Whom did you see? Whither did you go first?

FRANK: To Bond Street; where I enquired at once for the Miss.

MISS PERCIVAL: What, that thing I saw at your Sister's?

FRANK: No; 'tis the eldest hopes that takes the rule. I told her, with a bow and a smile that went straight to her heart –

MISS PERCIVAL: Now don't be so conceited.

FRANK: That you begged the honour of all their company to a small, private party here, in Piccadilly, this evening.

MISS PERCIVAL: Does she not think me mad?

FRANK: She accepted the invitation with the most vulgar joy: and I doubt not would have been here ere now, had she not deemed it an happy opportunity to load her poor head with yet another tier of ornament: as if external weight were to make ballast for internal emptiness!

MISS PERCIVAL: But will the other come?

FRANK: They are all at her control, and dare no more disobey her than a fag his monitor.

MISS PERCIVAL: And the Tylneys?

FRANK: I then returned to Albermarle Street, where I found poor Jemima distracting her brain for some device to prevent Sir Marmaduke and Lady Wil from coming – they are gone to dine and had appointed to meet her and my Brother here this evening.

MISS PERCIVAL: But I hope she has taken no measure to that effect?

FRANK: No; I charged her to keep her own engagement, and to let them keep theirs; telling her, at the same time, that though the affair had been a little awkward at the moment, neither you nor I thought now anymore of our disappointment.

MISS PERCIVAL: Frank, I could kill you with pleasure! And – who else?

FRANK: My brother, from the moment he was awed out of your presence, has been employed in composing explanatory epistles to all the party. I found him in the act, and assured him he gave himself vastly too much consequence in addressing one of them to you, for that you had quite forgotten the transaction, and expected, as a thing of course, the pleasure of his company, with the rest of his family, here this evening.

MISS PERCIVAL: Admirable! I forgive you everything now. Let me but be the first to name and present his new bridal relations to Lady Wilhelmina, and I acquit Fortune of spite! O, if I can but see him and them as mortified as myself – I shall become quite easy.

FRANK: Well, now let us talk of another scheme, and arrange how to surprise them in a new manner.

MISS PERCIVAL: With all my heart.

FRANK: To astonish, to strike them dumb.

MISS PERCIVAL: Tell me how.

FRANK: To make all their hairs

'Like Quills upon the fretful Porcupine –'

MISS PERCIVAL: No, how, I say?

FRANK: Let us pretend, nay, insist, that you never thought of my Brother at all.

MISS PERCIVAL: Pho!

FRANK: That the whole was a blunder of Sir Marmaduke's.

MISS PERCIVAL: O, if you can throw anything upon Sir Marmaduke –

FRANK: Seconded by my dear Brother's own vanity and presumption.

MISS PERCIVAL: Ah, Frank! You are bent upon enchanting me! But how am I to do this?

FRANK: By publicly, and before them all, – giving your hand to his brother.

MISS PERCIVAL: You abominable wretch! how you disappoint and torment me!

FRANK: She calls me wretch! – I advance! *(Aside.)*

Enter a SERVANT.

SERVANT: Lord John Dervis desires to speak a word in great haste to Mr Cleveland.

MISS PERCIVAL: Send him away! Did I not charge you not to let any of those idle fools in?

SERVANT: He said it was about something of so much consequence –

FRANK: I'll run down, and dispatch him myself. Say I am coming.

Exit SERVANT.

MISS PERCIVAL: How can you suffer that Ideot to follow you?

FRANK: He's a good-natured fellow, I assure you. Empty and dull, to be sure, but a special good-natured fellow.

MISS PERCIVAL: Well, run and get rid of him.

FRANK: I go. – And yet, – might not his presence heighten the effect of the introductions?

MISS PERCIVAL: O, ay, true; bring him up. I shall have them all shewn into this room.

Exit FRANK.

I won't receive the fool myself, however.

Exit. Re-enter FRANK, with LORD JOHN.

LORD JOHN: O the D–l, don't bring me here. I hate company.

FRANK: We shall be quite alone. But what's the matter? Has anything happened?

LORD JOHN: I want to speak to you deucedly. What a plague I've had to trace you! Why did not you dine at Club?

FRANK: Particular business. But what's the distress, Lord John?

LORD JOHN: Why I'll tell you. I can't think where the D–l to go tonight.

FRANK: Why what's the matter with the Opera?

LORD JOHN: Sick as a dog of it.

FRANK: I'll cut you out some work to do for me, then. You may serve me essentially.

LORD JOHN: What, write another letter, I suppose? I'll be hanged if I do, though!

FRANK: No; that affair's at an end. It did not take.

LORD JOHN: I'm glad of it for giving me that bore of a letter to write. I have been yawning ever since. And what hast got into thy head now, Franciscus?

FRANK: A prize, my dear Lord John, of the first magnitude. The daintiest monied Girl of the Day.

LORD JOHN: What! Matrimony again? O the D–l! nothing better than that?

FRANK: Peculiar circumstances give me the temerity to attempt what, but an hour ago, I should have thought as much above my reach as the Sun. But hush! – Wait a moment.

Enter MISS PERCIVAL.

MISS PERCIVAL: They are come. What shall I do with them till the Tylneys arrive?

FRANK: Let them amuse themselves with gaping about the rooms.

MISS PERCIVAL: You don't suppose I shall undertake to entertain them?

FRANK: By no means. Let us all be at our ease. Whatever we do they will conclude to be the high ton, and consider as a favour.

MISS PERCIVAL: I shall not take the smallest notice of them till I can make them of some use. I hate trouble.

FRANK: My own motto! It is amazing what a congeniality of sentiment is perpetually breaking forth between us.

MISS PERCIVAL: No nonsense, I beg. I am in a dreadful ill humour.

FRANK: So am I. Our sympathy encreases every moment.

MISS PERCIVAL: I shall begin to detest you, Frank, if you go on so. *(Throwing herself into a great chair.)*

FRANK: There, then, our congeniality will end, for I feel myself beginning to adore you. *(Throws himself into another, which he draws next to hers.)*

LORD JOHN: I don't know what the D–l to do with myself. *(Throws himself full length upon a sofa.)*

Enter MRS. WATTS, and MISS WATTS, richly dressed.

MRS. WATTS: Dears, what a pretty house! Dears, if ever I see the like! Only look! But I wonder where's the lady that the Gentleman said invited us, that she don't come to welcome us.

MISS WATTS: La, ma', don't talk so loud. Don't you see there's Company? You always behave so vulgar!

MRS. WATTS: Dears, so there is! And all sot down! I'm sure I never see 'em, or I should not have come in so rude. *(She makes three low Courtsies.)*

MISS WATTS: La, Ma', that stiff courtsie's quite old-fashioned now. Look at mine. I could make ten before you've done one.

MRS. WATTS: Why, my dear, I must make 'em one a piece, you know.

MISS PERCIVAL: *(To FRANK.)* What curiosities! But I don't see the Gentoo?

FRANK: Nor I. I begin to fear she won't come.

MISS WATTS: Come this way Ma', for here's Pa' with old Tibbs.

Enter MR. WATTS and MR. TIBBS bowing low.

MISS PERCIVAL: Heavens! here are my eternal Wigs.

FRANK: But I see nothing of my little Cit. She has certainly refused to come.

MISS PERCIVAL: Undone, undone! – If I do not make her partake of my spleen, I shall never know peace again. Dear Frank, contrive but to bring her, and command me evermore. *(They whisper.)*

MR WATTS: Now you'll believe me another time, Cousin Tibbs! For all we've been making all them bows, they all sit as kimposed upon their cheres, as if we was no better than a mere dumb cretur come in.

MR TIBBS: Fegs, they shall bestir themselves a little, though, before I'll bob so for 'em agen. My neck's no looser than theirs, I can tell 'em.

MISS PERCIVAL: *(To FRANK.)* Do you think that will do?

FRANK: Perfectly. So mysterious an entreaty cannot fail to bring her.

MISS PERCIVAL: Why then write it for me. She don't know my hand.

FRANK: If you want a secretary, Lord John's your man. Lord John, Miss Percival begs you'll write a note for her.

LORD JOHN: The D–l I will!

MISS PERCIVAL: I'll do it myself. *(Rises and passes by MR WATTS, while he is bowing to her.)*

Exit.

MR WATTS: The civiler one is, the ruder they be! You'd never believe what a push she gave me in going by.

MR TIBBS: Yes, but I can, though, for she's the same lady as squealed so at me in Kinsington Gardens. And the whole is all no how as one may say; inviting a body when there's never a mistress of the house, nor nobody to go to, nor to make one a dish of tea.

LORD JOHN: I wish, Frank, you'd tell me what to do. *(He re-takes his seat on the sofa.)*

FRANK: I will. I will. *(To MISS WATTS.)* How do do, ma'am? Pray will you give me leave to enquire why Miss Percival has not the honour of seeing Miss Elizabeth tonight?

MISS WATTS: Sir, she's got the headache.

MRS WATTS: She's a little bit fertigued, sir, I take it, for she's come from Indy this morning.

MR TIBBS: Good lauk, Tom, look at them fine gentlemen! One's lying all along, as if he was sick a bed; and t'other's gaping at Cousin Peg, as if he was going to take a nap full in her face!

MR WATTS: Well, if they an't both the two gentlemen of Betsey's acquaintance at the Hitel! I'm sure, sir, *(To LORD JOHN.)* I did not know you. Pray, sir, may I make free –

LORD JOHN: Umph?

MR WATTS: I say, sir, may I make free –

LORD JOHN: *(Affecting not to hear him.)* Frank, will you step with me this way. I want to speak with you plaguely. *(he sings to himself.)* La, la, la, la, lall – By your permission, sir!

Pushes past MR WATTS, and exit singing.

MR WATTS: This t'other'll be civil enough, I suppose; for he's one of the Muster Clevelands as had a mind to my Darter. Pray, sir, – *(To FRANK.)*

FRANK: Sir, your very most obedient! Fal de ral.

Rises abruptly, humming an air, and exits without looking at him.

MR WATTS: They all treat me alike, you see! Ah Cousin Tibbs! Never begin to set up for a gentleman in the middle of life!

MR TIBBS: Well, if it don't make my blood boil! What right have they to be deaf more than another man?

MRS WATTS: Dears, my dear, only look, there's coming a purdigus fine lady, as I dares to say is the mistress of the house.

MISS WATTS: La, so there is! And a gentleman with her. Let's talk a little free and pelite with 'em.

Enter LADY WILHELMINA and SIR MARMADUKE.

LADY WILHELMINA: Is it not somewhat strange, Sir Marmaduke, that there is no-one to receive me; a young person of the rank of Miss Percival should – Bless me! what people are these?

SIR MARMADUKE: I can't imagine: unless those – *(Pointing to MR WATTS and MR TIBBS.)* are two new men out of livery.

LADY WILHELMINA: Impossible she can have chosen two such grotesque figures. And look at those strange Women! how extraordinary! I can't turn my head round, but that odd body makes me a courtsie!

MRS WATTS: Dears, my dear, I wish she'd receive us, like; for I'll be whipt if I can think of a word to say for a beginning.

MISS WATTS: Why, ask her if she's going to Rinelur. That's the genteel thing to talk about in genteel Company.

MRS WATTS: I will, my dear. Pray, good lady, may you be going to Rinelur tonight?

LADY WILHELMINA: Sir Marmaduke!

SIR MARMADUKE: Lady Wil?

LADY WILHELMINA: Did anybody – speak to Me?

MRS WATTS: Yes, it was me, my good lady, as spoke.

LADY WILHELMINA: How incomprehensible! people of such a stamp to enquire into my engagements! what can Miss Percival mean by exposing me to such extraordinary familiarity?

MRS WATTS: She seems mighty pertickler, my dear, she's put me quite out.

MISS WATTS: La, Ma', nobody'll be pelite to you, if you're so over and above civil. They find you out for a low person directly. See how I do! – I think, mem, it's rather a hot evening, mem? Can you be so obliging, mem, without undressing yourself –

LADY WILHELMINA: Undressing myself!

MISS WATTS: As just to lend me a long pin, mem, if you've one to spare; for my Feathers feel so loose –

LADY WILHELMINA: How singular!

SIR MARMADUKE: Some freaks; take no notice of them.

MISS WATTS: They look as if they thought we were just a set of nobodys.

Enter MISS PERCIVAL.

MISS PERCIVAL: Lady Wilhelmina! I did not know your La'ship was come. How are you Sir Marmaduke? I make no apology, Lady Wilhelmina, for having left you alone with so agreeable a party. How happy you must have been!

LADY WILHELMINA: Madam?

SIR MARMADUKE: She's certainly crazy! I wish the deeds had been signed for my mortgage. *(Aside.)*

MRS WATTS: I'm sure, ma'am, that's very genteel of you, what you're so kind to say of our being so agreeable. – Where's your courtsie my dear? *(Curtseying low.)*

MISS WATTS: La, Ma', don't you see?

MR WATTS: *(To MR TIBBS.)* This is the first of all the gentry as has ever said such a word as my being agreeable. I'm sure, ma'am, *(Bowing.)* –

MISS PERCIVAL: What pretty people! But don't I interrupt you, Lady Wilhelmina? Do be sincere now; don't I break in upon your little family chat?

LADY WILHELMINA: Miss Percival! This exceeds whatever I have yet met with for incredibility! An Earl's daughter – Lady Wilhelmina Tylney, classed with persons of such a description!

MR TIBBS: Harkee, Tom! If this is the best manners your fine folks has got to shew us, they may keep them for one another. They won't do for me.

Exit. Enter CLEVELAND.

LADY WILHELMINA: O my good Cleveland, how I revive in seeing you!

MISS PERCIVAL: Mr Cleveland! how kind is this call!

CLEVELAND: Kind, madam?

MISS PERCIVAL: Unless, indeed, you knew the party you were to meet. O you wicked Creature!

CLEVELAND: What party, madam? – Heavens! *(Aside.)*

SIR MARMADUKE: Let me speak to you first, Nephew.

LADY WILHELMINA: Sir Marmaduke, I am quite uneasy for a consultation with him.

SIR MARMADUKE: I don't meddle with your uneasiness, Lady Wil; but I have something I want to say to him myself; and I never defer my own business. Come this way, Nephew.

Exit.

MISS WATTS: La, what a smart beau!

MISS PERCIVAL: Tell me the truth, now; had not some report reached you that this company would be here?

CLEVELAND: Upon my honour, madam, I – I –

MISS PERCIVAL: O bless me! perhaps you don't know them then? What a mistake I have been guilty of! however, I must Positively make you acquainted with one another. Give me leave, Mr – Mr – how shockingly stupid I am! I can't for my life recollect this gentleman's name!

MR WATTS: Thomas Watts, ma'am. That's my name.

MISS PERCIVAL: Mr Thomas Watts! – Mr Cleveland, let me have the honour of presenting you to each other.

CLEVELAND: *(Bowing, and turning aside.)* Confusion! What demon has been at work to bring them hither! *(Aside.)*

MISS PERCIVAL: Permit me, now, to have the honour of introducing you to the ladies – Mrs – Mrs I've lost that name again!

CLEVELAND: What impertinent affectation! *(Aside.)*

MISS PERCIVAL: O! Watts – ay, Watts. Mrs Watts, will you allow me the pleasure of presenting Mr Cleveland to you?

MRS WATTS: I a'n't no peticler objection, as I know of, mem, if the gentleman's none. *(Making sundry formal courtsies.)*

LADY WILHELMINA: My good Cleveland, approach this way. Do you understand anything of all this? Can you unravel it? Inviting Me to such unheard of persons?

CLEVELAND: Indeed I – I – I –

LADY WILHELMINA: Persons one would rather be buried alive than ever speak to?

CLEVELAND: Ma'am I – I – really –

LADY WILHELMINA: I don't wonder at your distress; but let me recommend it to you, to use your influence with Miss Percival to put a period to such fancies.

CLEVELAND: My influence, Madam? Has not Miss Percival informed you –

LADY WILHELMINA: Who can they possibly be? Where can she have picked them up?

MISS WATTS: La, I thought we was going to be introduced all round! I don't know what I'm to be left out for! *(Aside.)*

MISS PERCIVAL: Come, Mrs – Mrs – Mrs Watts, come and sit upon this sofa with Lady Wilhelmina. I'm sure you must have a thousand things to say to one another.

MRS WATTS: Lady? – O laws! Who'd have thought of that! I've been speaking to a Lady! – I'm sure ma'am, I never guessed at the lady's being a Lady! *(Courtsying again lower and lower.)*

MISS PERCIVAL: Come Lady Wilhelmina, –

LADY WILHELMINA: Is it possible, Miss Percival, you can suppose I shall trouble this – gentlewoman to sit by Me? A – gentlewoman I have so little probability of troubling again? And whom, certainly, I never had the – accident of meeting before?

MISS PERCIVAL: Never meeting before? My stars, Lady Wilhelmina! you seem to know nothing of your nearest connexions.

LADY WILHELMINA: Connexions, Miss Percival?

MISS PERCIVAL: Nay, if the alliance is a secret …

LADY WILHELMINA: The alliance? What pleasantry is this? Can you help me, Mr Cleveland, to comprehend what Miss Percival would say?

CLEVELAND: Me, madam? I – I – I – O that I were in Calcutta! *(Aside.)*

MISS PERCIVAL: I must speak to Mr Cleveland myself. Pray –

CLEVELAND: I entreat to – to – to take my leave. A particular engagement.

MISS PERCIVAL: No; come hither, man, and don't mar your own good fortune. I have sent for you – Listen, I say! – merely to give you a meeting with the fair lady of your choice. *(In a low voice.)*

CLEVELAND: Madam?

MISS PERCIVAL: Am I not explicit? I have invited you solely to have the pleasure of procuring you a tête-à-tête with Miss Watts.

CLEVELAND: I am so astonished – so –

Enter ELIZA unobserved by CLEVELAND.

MISS PERCIVAL: She is come at last! *(Aside.)* You won't see her, then, perhaps?

CLEVELAND: Not see her?

MISS PERCIVAL: And won't own yourself obliged to me? *(Holding out her hand.)*

CLEVELAND: *(Kissing it.)* Ah, madam! exquisitely!

ELIZA: Heavens! for this am I forced hither? *(Aside.)*

CLEVELAND: *(Not seeing her.)* Such unexpected goodness – I want words –

ELIZA: Can I bear this? Perfidious, faithless Cleveland! *(Aside.)*

MISS PERCIVAL: Well, go quietly into that next room, and eat custards, till I have hussled away all others. No thanks, man. *(Pushes him out.)* Miss Elizabeth! This is extremely good indeed.

ELIZA: I knew not how, madam, to resist the urgency of your note – though why I am summoned –

MISS PERCIVAL: You don't seem well?

ELIZA: My head – a little – aches –

LADY WILHELMINA: Is not this the young lady I had the pleasure to see this afternoon in Albermarle Street? *(ELIZA curtseys.)* Allow me to enquire after your health; and pray, ma'am, *(In a low voice.)* – suffer me to ask if you can conjecture who these singular persons are?

ELIZA: Madam!

LADY WILHELMINA: How can Miss Percival have gotten them together? I am sure you never can have seen such before. An elegant young woman like you must be offended –

ELIZA: Pardon me, madam – I am not quite well – I must beg a glass of water – O Cleveland! are you a party in this insult to all my feelings? *(Aside.)*

MISS WATTS: La, what can have brought Eliziana?

MRS WATTS: Why Betsey, my dear, why how come you to come?

MISS PERCIVAL: *(To ELIZA.)* In that Boudoir you can ring and order what you please.

Exit ELIZA, eagerly followed by MRS and MISS WATTS.

MR WATTS: I should like to know what has brought Bet, too. Ladies, your servant.

Exit.

MISS PERCIVAL: Delightful creatures! Do now, let me wish you joy, Lady Wilhelmina. You must like them so amazingly. How I hope I shall see you all together some evening at Ranelagh!

LADY WILHELMINA: I trust I shall never so far forget what is due to my rank in life, Miss Percival, as to lose my temper; but you will have the goodness to dispense with my remaining any longer to be affronted in this extraordinary manner with persons of such a Stamp.

Exit.

MISS PERCIVAL: How deliciously she is worked! It is balm to me to behold her. And now –

Enter SIR MARMADUKE.

Sir Marmaduke!

SIR MARMADUKE: You make me happy my dear Miss Percival, by your call. You have been so surrounded by – new friends, I hardly dared approach you. Where's my Nephew?

MISS PERCIVAL: My dear Sir Marmaduke, our love of each other's society is, I am sure, reciprocal; and so perfectly am I convinced of your kindness for me –

SIR MARMADUKE: You do me but justice.

MISS PERCIVAL: So satisfied of the disinterested view with which you promote my union with your Nephew –

SIR MARMADUKE: My dear young lady, your confidence makes me happy.

MISS PERCIVAL: That I make not the smallest scruple to tell you – I am now wholly resolved against that mortgage engagement.

SIR MARMADUKE: I thank you – What? – How? –

MISS PERCIVAL: I withdraw my consent to it. That's all.

SIR MARMADUKE: Withdraw your consent to it? And pray – Why?

MISS PERCIVAL: I've changed my mind.

SIR MARMADUKE: Changed your mind? But why? Pray why?

MISS PERCIVAL: I really can't tell. However, it will make no change, I know, in you. I feel equally sure of your desire to make us happy – and – of your Lincolnshire Estate.

Exit.

SIR MARMADUKE: A little vixen! Not pay off my mortgage? A little D–l! Give them my Lincolnshire Estate, indeed? Not a sixpence of it!

Re-enter MISS PERCIVAL, with CLEVELAND.

MISS PERCIVAL: I have dispersed all troublesome spectators now, but Sir Marmaduke; and you may dispatch him, while I prepare the young lady for the tête-à-tête I have promised you.

CLEVELAND: What thanks can I offer you?

MISS PERCIVAL exits by another door.

Sir Marmaduke, may I seize this little moment to open to you my situation?

SIR MARMADUKE: I enter into nothing that don't concern me, Nephew: but if 'tis about the Lincolnshire Estate – I must frankly tell you – I can't part with it.

CLEVELAND: Sir!

SIR MARMADUKE: I am very sorry, my dear Cleveland; but a man's own affairs must first be consulted; and the times are so bad – one can but barely live, however careful. You are a young man, though, and if the loss of the Lincolnshire Estate throws any obstacles in your way – What hinders a little voyage back to India to mend your fortune?

CLEVELAND: A little voyage, sir, to the East Indies?

SIR MARMADUKE: Why what's half a dozen years, or so, in the life of a young man? I hate fuss about common casualties. No fuss, I tell you, Nephew! no difficulties about trifles.

Exit.

CLEVELAND: Alas! how unhappy a turn for affairs to take, at the moment Eliza seems so hurt or so offended! Can I sue back her favour, implore her returning tenderness and confidence, when a bankrupt in all but love? No! her decision must be noble, unsolicited, and prompt, or the cruel alternative of Sir Marmaduke must indeed be put in practice.

Enter MISS PERCIVAL.

MISS PERCIVAL: Now then, sir, I hope to deserve the gratitude you profess, and to repay, in part, what so amply I owe! behold – *(Leading in MISS WATTS.)*

CLEVELAND: Who, madam?

MISS PERCIVAL: Miss Watts, sir!

CLEVELAND: Where, madam?

MISS PERCIVAL: Here! – And now I leave you to the enjoyment I have promised of an uninterrupted tête-à-tête.

Exit.

MISS WATTS: La, how droll! He's fell in love with me without knowing my name! It must be love at first sight, I think. *(Aside.)*

CLEVELAND: What execrable vengeance is this! *(Aside.)*

MISS WATTS: He looks quite the gentleman; but it's odd he don't begin. *(Aside.)*

CLEVELAND: What am I to do now? How cruel is an angry woman! *(Aside.)*

MISS WATTS: I dare say he'll say something pretty, when he's got it ready. *(Aside.)*

CLEVELAND: Madam, I – my confusion –

MISS WATTS: La! he's quite the lover. *(Aside.)*

CLEVELAND: This mistake –

MISS WATTS: Mistake, sir?

CLEVELAND: It is I believe – a near relation, a Sister, I imagine – of yours, that Miss Percival –

MISS WATTS: A sister? La! What, Eliziana?

CLEVELAND: Yes, madam, Miss Elizabeth. If I might be allowed – a short conference with her – how inexpressibly, should I be obliged!

MISS WATTS: O la, sir, pray let it be as long as you please! Don't make it short for me, I beg! I'm sure I don't care. I'll call her myself to you. *(Calling out the door.)* Here, Sister Eliziana! *(Aside.)* I'm glad it wa'n't me, I'm sure, for I hate Lovers. *(Calling.)* Sister, I say!

Exit.

CLEVELAND: How does my heart, how does every pulse acknowledge her power, and tremble at the use she may make of it! She comes!

Enter ELIZA.

This, at least, is condescending.

ELIZA: I would not refuse this once, sir, to converse a few moments with one whom –

CLEVELAND: This once, madam?

ELIZA: What more than once can I accord, or can you desire, in this altered state of things? Altered irreversibly!

CLEVELAND: Enough! Altered, indeed! Pardon the temerity
of this last intrusion. I should not have presumed to urge it,
had I not imagined it possible some elucidation – but I was
mistaken. You have gathered, I conclude, the history of my
recall, and its consequences?

ELIZA: Yes, sir; I have gathered all I now ever wish to know.

CLEVELAND: I have only, then, madam, to supplicate you
would believe that I have not entreated for this short
interview –

ELIZA: It cannot be too brief!

CLEVELAND: With any formed design to harass you by
solicitations –

ELIZA: Spare the assurance, sir! they have not been numbered
in my expectations.

CLEVELAND: Ah, rather spare, Eliza, this cold cruelty! let me
not, however, stray into reproach, for to that I would owe
no obligation. Take therefore back all engagement! I must
not offend you by acknowledgements for what is past – O
that as readily I could command forgetfulness as silence!
Adieu, Eliza! – My farewell, since you ordain so, must be
brief – but who can tell my wounded soul when its effects
may know a term? *(Going.)*

Enter JEMIMA.

JEMIMA: My Brother!

CLEVELAND: Stay me not!

Exit.

JEMIMA: What can this mean?

ELIZA: I know not! I am all astonishment. Is it for him to shew
resentment? Is it his to speak of a wounded soul?

JEMIMA: Has he not explained to you his situation?

ELIZA: Has it not explained itself? Or has any
misapprehension involved my judgement in errour? Ah,
Miss Cleveland!

JEMIMA: Let us seek a quiet room – for here we shall be broken in upon every moment and permit me, dear madam, to state to you a few simple facts.

ELIZA: Will they bring home mistake to me – and to Cleveland honour?

JEMIMA: Will you pardon me if I say yes?

ELIZA: Pardon? I shall contest with him to which you are most a sister.

Exeunt. Enter MR TIBBS with cakes in each hand.

MR TIBBS: Well I can't but say I'm rather in better humour since I've made free with all them tidbits. I've put myself at the tip of the mode for that; and I can't but say I like it well enough. I suppose I've eat me clear a pastry cook's shop.

Enter MISS WATTS.

What? Cousin Peg! why I suppose, now nobody's by, a body may ask you how you do?

MISS WATTS: *(After looking around.)* How do do, Cozen Joel?

MR TIBBS: What think you of this purdigious fine quality breeding? Walking off one by one, without never a word, except turning up their noses? If this here behaviour's what they call the thing, it's none so difficult. I warrant I could do it as well as they.

MISS WATTS: You? O, to be sure! You're very like to a person of qualitee!

MR TIBBS: Nay, I'll bet you sixpence I can do after the manner of that lord thing-um, and that t'other fine mister, as was here just now, so as you should not know one of us from t'other.

MISS WATTS: Don't vaunt you so, Cousin Joel. Here comes that grand lady.

MR TIBBS: Vaunt me? Have you a mind I should try?

MISS WATTS: You durst not!

MR TIBBS: Durst not! Fegs, you shall soon see that! What need I care?

Enter LADY WILHELMINA.

LADY WILHELMINA: How enormously unfortunate that the servants are not to be found! I know not which way to turn my eyes to avoid some disagreeable object.

MR TIBBS: How do do?

LADY WILHELMINA: What?

MR TIBBS: I hope you are confounded well?

LADY WILHELMINA: Heavens!

MR TIBBS: O the Doose, and the Devel, and the plague and consumed!

LADY WILHELMINA: What inscrutable effrontery! I'll look him into a statue. *(Fixes her eyes upon him and frowns.)*

MR TIBBS: How do, I say? *(Nodding familiarly.)*

LADY WILHELMINA: Dignity is lost upon such ignorance.

MR TIBBS: Tol de rol. O the Doose – *(Striding about ludicrously imitating LORD JOHN.)*

LADY WILHELMINA: This is a class of person beyond any I have met with yet!

MR TIBBS: O the Divil! *(Throws himself full length upon the sofa.)*

MISS WATTS: He! He!

LADY WILHELMINA: What can that vulgar thing find to laugh at? But low people are beneath notice. I'll sit down myself, and force their retreat by silent contempt. What do I see? A person of that description presuming to lie down upon a sofa? A sofa which I had thoughts of occupying myself!

Enter SIR MARMADUKE.

LADY WILHELMINA: O Sir Marmaduke! I have received an affront past all comparison! I am on the very point of fainting.

SIR MARMADUKE: I don't meddle with that, Lady Wilhelmina. Would you believe Miss Percival has thought proper to order my servants to the public house, because forsooth, of the storm!

LADY WILHELMINA: The storm – Is there a storm? O how shall I have the courage to get home?

SIR MARMADUKE: Heigh – Who's that fellow lying upon the sofa?

MISS WATTS: He! He!

Enter MRS WATTS.

MRS WATTS: *(To MISS WATTS.)* Dear, my dear, so you're here at last? My feet hurt me so. If I don't sit down –

MR TIBBS: Tol de rol. *(Sings.)*

MRS WATTS: Dears! What a sight is here! Out upon you, Joel!

MRS WATTS: Is that your manners? Singing without being asked?

MISS WATTS: *(Whispering.)* La, Ma', what do you let people know you know him for?

MRS WATTS: Why, what right has he to take that fine couch to hisself?

SIR MARMADUKE: What a crew! *(Aside.)*

MRS WATTS: Why Joel, I say, an't you ashamed?

MR TIBBS: Hay?

MRS WATTS: Why don't you offer the seat to the lady?

MR TIBBS: What?

MRS WATTS: What! What! Don't you know English, man?

MR TIBBS: English? O consumed!

MRS WATTS: Dears, if you a'n't enough to turn one's brain! One might as well talk to the post.

SIR MARMADUKE: Pray, madam, will you give me leave to ask – do you happen to know who that gentleman is?

MISS WATTS: *(Whispering.)* Say no, Ma'!

MRS WATTS: Not in the least, sir. Some poor low cretur, I suppose.

MR TIBBS: *(Starting up.)* Some poor low cretur? Fegs, that's pretty high! Why I'm afeard, Cousin Aylce, it's you has lost your wits!

MISS WATTS: Come this way, Ma'!

Exit hastily.

MRS WATTS: Well, my dear, only don't go so purdigious fast.

Exit.

MR TIBBS: O fegs, but you shall hear me!

Exit.

LADY WILHELMINA: Why do you not speak to Miss Percival yourself, Sir Marmaduke, upon this singular proceeding?

SIR MARMADUKE: Why what harm does it do to me?

Enter JEMIMA.

JEMIMA: My dear Uncle, my dear Lady Wilhelmina, I come to you with a narrative – and a proposition – upon which all my Brother's happiness depends.

SIR MARMADUKE: What, about my Lincolnshire Estate, I suppose? But I can't part with it now. I want it myself. And as to his happiness, he'll never be happy while he lives, if he lets himself be ruffled by every petty disappointment. He should command more fortitude.

JEMIMA: But, sir, if the mortgage –

SIR MARMADUKE: Don't mention it! 'Tis the cursedest provocation I ever met with. I lose all temper at it.

JEMIMA: But if a young lady should suddenly appear, still richer than Miss Percival, and still more attached to my Brother, who would instantly acquiesce in that condition –

SIR MARMADUKE: How –? What ? – Is there anybody will pay off my mortgage?

JEMIMA: There is. A young lady the most amiable; by whose desire I have written the generous proposition to my Brother, whom I expect every instant –

LADY WILHELMINA: But who is she? What is her Birth?

SIR MARMADUKE: O, hang her Birth! What is her fortune?

Enter CLEVELAND.

CLEVELAND: Jemima! – Is this possible? – my Uncle – Lady Wilhelmina –

SIR MARMADUKE: I don't understand a word of the matter. I have not seen one deed relative to what she is worth.

LADY WILHELMINA: I don't comprehend a syllable. I have heard nothing of her genealogy.

JEMIMA: She is here! come this way dear madam – and Sir Marmaduke – and let me unravel the history before you meet.

Exeunt. Enter ELIZA.

CLEVELAND: Generous Eliza! And can it be after a parting so abrupt, so desperate, that you deign thus sweetly to call me back to life – to love – to yourself?

ELIZA: Can you blame me for that parting? – No, Cleveland, no! when you think how cruel a combination of circumstances conspired to alarm and make me wretched –

CLEVELAND: Wretched? Dear, loved Eliza! You permit me then, to hope the separation with which this eventful day has been teeming was not dreaded by me alone?

ELIZA: Ah no! why should I try to disguise, that from the moment I consented to give you my hand, you became the master of my happiness?

Enter JEMIMA, followed by SIR MARMADUKE.

JEMIMA: My dear Brother, Sir Marmaduke complies; and but that Lady Wilhelmina is just now cruelly disturbed –

SIR MARMADUKE: And what have I to do with that? Come hither, my dear Nephew; I'll tell thee what. Since the young lady's so generous – what a happy young rascal thou art! – since she's so generous, I say, why – sooner than lose sight of thee again, – I'll –

CLEVELAND: What, dear sir?

SIR MARMADUKE: Accept her proposition for paying off my mortgage – and make over to thee my Lincolnshire Estate.

CLEVELAND: This goodness, my dear Uncle, would exceed even my desire, but that I hope from it the entire consent of my Eliza's friends.

ELIZA: 'Tis that alone which, to me, can give value to your acquisitions. They are now in the next room, hasten, I beseech you, and acquaint them with Sir Marmaduke's munificence.

SIR MARMADUKE: I'll go myself, young lady.

ELIZA: How good! How kind!

SIR MARMADUKE: They'll be sure, else to make some blunder about my mortgage. *(Aside.)*

Exit ELIZA, between SIR MARMADUKE and CLEVELAND, with JEMIMA. Enter MISS PERCIVAL, LORD JOHN, and FRANK CLEVELAND.

MISS PERCIVAL: What can be the meaning of this? They seem all reconciled and delighted!

LORD JOHN: O the D–l!

FRANK: Yes, yes; all is over, and they are completely happy.

MISS PERCIVAL: How abominable!

FRANK: We're in a shocking way here, Miss Percival!

LORD JOHN: Confoundedly shocking!

MISS PERCIVAL: How? What do you mean?

FRANK: All in the background!

LORD JOHN: Deucedly back!

MISS PERCIVAL: Who, I say, who?

FRANK: My dear madam – you and I!

MISS PERCIVAL: Impertinent fop!

FRANK: Adorable Creature! – Ah madam, raillery apart, what spirit would you preserve – and O what bliss might you bestow, by nipping in the bud the triumph for which malice is preparing!

MISS PERCIVAL: What triumph?

FRANK: Lady Wilhelmina, finding no one here but Lord John whose rank permitted a vent to her indignation; – Lord John, – step this way. Miss Percival will be curious to hear Lady Wil's rhapsody from yourself.

LORD JOHN: O the Deuce! She's consumedly tift. She dooms poor Cleveland to the bastinado. What, says she, shall a young lady of the rank of Miss Percival honour him with her passion –

MISS PERCIVAL: How? Passion?

LORD JOHN: And shall he reject her? –

MISS PERCIVAL: Reject her? Intolerable! – I shall die of this insolence! *(Sitting down.)*

FRANK: *(Kneeling.)* Ah! by one generous stroke disperse its arrows.

MISS PERCIVAL: Go – Go!

LORD JOHN: And for a young Cit! says she.

MISS PERCIVAL: Monstrous!

Enter SIR MARMADUKE, CLEVELAND, ELIZA and JEMIMA.

FRANK: *(Rising.)* How exulting they look!

MISS PERCIVAL: Nay, what do you rise just now for?

FRANK: *(Kneeling, and seizing her hand.)* Enchanting Fair One! so you permit, then, my adoration?

MISS PERCIVAL: No, no!

SIR MARMADUKE: What's this? Is Frank begging pardon for his Brother?

CLEVELAND: I trust, Miss Percival, –

MISS PERCIVAL: Dear sir, have you the goodness to be uneasy for me?

FRANK: Or the grace to conclude no Cleveland could be favoured by a fair lady, but yourself?

ALL: How?

FRANK: See your mistake, good Brother, learn to be modest – and resemble me! *(Kissing MISS PERCIVAL's hand.)*

MISS PERCIVAL: Be quiet, you shocking Creature!

JEMIMA: Ah, dear Miss Percival, still, then, may I retain a Sister?

SIR MARMADUKE: Bravo, Frank! – They'll both be ruined in half a year: however, that's no business of mine. *(Aside.)*

Enter LADY WILHELMINA, MR, MRS and MISS WATTS, and MR TIBBS. LADY WILHELMINA brushes past MR TIBBS to enter first.

LADY WILHELMINA: You will have the goodness, sir, to make way.

MR TIBBS: O yes, ma'am. I never force my company. I like nobody that don't like me.

LADY WILHELMINA: Were such vulgar wretches ever born before? Anything ever seen so disagreeable? *(Half aside.)*

MR TIBBS: *(Listening.)* O yes, ma'am! as to that the World's full of disagreeable people. *(Staring her full in her face.)*

MR WATTS: *(To ELIZA.)* Well, Bet, my dear, as the Baronight will come down so handsome –

MRS WATTS: Dears, Tommy how rude you speak! You should say –

MISS WATTS: La, Ma', you let nobody speak but yourself! Sister Eliziana –

LADY WILHELMINA: Surely, Sir Marmaduke, you have not accommodated yourself with a person descended from such a tribe?

CLEVELAND: Ah Madam – look not at the root, but the flower!

LADY WILHELMINA: I can make no compromise, sir! She would ally us with the City! – O Sir Marmaduke! I shall die if you consent, I shall die!

SIR MARMADUKE: That's your affair Lady Wil.

LORD JOHN: Die? O the D–l!

ELIZA: Ah! Cleveland! Were you less dear to me, how could I have courage to meet a prejudice so chillingly unkind, so indiscriminately unjust?

CLEVELAND: My Eliza, while your delicacy has had a charm which has distanced all the allurements of flattery, all the attractions of partiality, let me claim, from your true greatness of mind, a cool superiority to resentment against those who, forgetting that Merit is limited to no spot, and confined to no Class, affect to despise and degrade the natives of that noble Metropolis, which is the source of our Splendour, the seat of integrity, the foster Mother of Benevolence and Charity, and the Pride of the British Empire.

FINIS.